Reflexivity

The post-modern predicament

D1535069

PLATE 2

Reflexivity

The post-modern predicament

HILARY LAWSON

OPEN ✳ COURT

La Salle, Illinois

OPEN COURT and the above logo are registered
in the U.S. Patent & Trademark Office.

OC 883   10 9 8 7 6 5 4 3 2 1

ISBN: 0-8126-9011-7

Published by arrangement with Hutchinson Publishing Group Ltd.

First published 1985

© Hilary Lawson 1985

Set in Baskerville by Folio Photosetting, Bristol

Printed and bound in Great Britain by
Anchor Brendon Ltd.,
Tiptree, Essex

Library of Congress Cataloging in Publication Data

Lawson, Hilary.
Reflexivity: Truth and Test.

1. Self-knowledge, Theory of.   I. Title.
BD450.L363   1985   121   85–18757

Contents

Editors' foreword

During most of the twentieth century, philosophers in the English-speaking world have had only partial and fleeting glimpses of the work of their counterparts in continental Europe. In the main, English-language philosophy has been dominated by the exacting ideals of conceptual analysis and even of formal logic, while 'continental philosophy' has ventured into extensive substantive discussions of literary, historical, psycho-analytic and political themes. With relatively few exceptions, the relations between the two traditions have been largely uncomprehending and hostile.

In recent years, however, continental writers such as Heidegger, Adorno, Sartre, de Beauvoir, Habermas, Foucault, Althusser, Lacan and Derrida have been widely read in English translation, setting the terms of theoretical debate in such fields as literature, social theory, cultural studies, marxism, and feminism. The suspicions of the analytical philosophers have not, however, been pacified; and the import of such continental philosophy has mostly been isolated from original philosophical work in English.

PROBLEMS OF MODERN EUROPEAN THOUGHT series is intended to help break down this isolation. The books in the series will be original philosophical essays in their own right, from authors familiar with the procedures of analytical philosophy. Each book will present a well-defined range of themes from continental philosophy, and will presuppose little, if any formal philosophical training of its readers.

Alan Montefiore
Jonathan Rée

Preface

This book is about reflexivity. It is about the post-modern crisis. It is about Nietzsche, Heidegger and Derrida. However, it does not seek to present a fixed and final account. Its claims, *including this one*, are not intended to be held, they do not attempt to stand.

There are those who seek, under the banner of structuralism, post-structuralism, or deconstruction, an interpretive method and a philosophical theory. Already such theories are beginning to be taught in universities and colleges. For the present these are often regarded as being subversive, but no doubt the time will come when they are part of established opinion. However, we should remind both those who endorse this fashion, and those who regard it as pernicious, of a quotation from *Thus Spake Zarathustra* – the book Nietzsche regarded as his most profound. At one point, Zarathustra, the mouthpiece for Nietzsche's philosophy, says to his disciples: 'Verily I beseech you: depart from me, and guard yourself against Zarathustra! And better still be ashamed of him! Perhaps he had deceived you . . .'.

Before we respond by removing Nietzsche's texts from our bookshelves, or more subtly by reinterpreting Nietzsche as an adherent of dissimulation and untruth, we should reflect that the advice given in the quotation is also part of the deception. To guard ourselves against Nietzsche is to carry out his advice: to depart from Nietzsche is thus also to follow him – for he has told us to do this very thing. For similar reasons one cannot in any straightforward sense be a follower of Derrida. To express it in this way, 'in any straightforward sense', however, is to disguise the problem. It is not sufficient simply to qualify and avoid assertion, for if one is sympathetic to these philosophers one is forced both to assert that their theories are true, and at the same time to deny them.

This difficulty exemplifies a form of reflexivity. On its own it does not indicate a problem of any notable significance, but it does show that one effect of reflexivity is to place in question the way in which the text is to be approached. A text written in the light of reflexivity is, at a certain level, evasive (even when it appears dogmatic). For those acquainted with analytic philosophy, therefore, the style of this book will at times seem foreign. However, reflexivity is not a concern of continental philosophers that can be safely disregarded, for parallel problems can be found at the core of analytic philosophy, as well as many other disciplines.

While this book may be about reflexivity, it cannot itself avoid the problems it seeks to demonstrate. Nor can a self-conscious nod in this direction suffice to settle the matter. As Nietzsche might have said, reflexivity is the burden that we can neither carry nor throw off. The following warning is not meant as a denial but as an indication that all is not quite what is seems. Let it be clear therefore, that the quotation from Nietzsche applies quite as much to this text, and to this preliminary bracket, as it does to the teachings of Zarathustra.

1

A new age . . . ?

The post-modern predicament is indeed one of crisis, a crisis of our truths, our values, our most cherished beliefs. A crisis that owes to reflexivity its origin, its necessity, and its force.

Reflexivity, as a turning back on oneself, a form of self-awareness, has been part of philosophy from its inception, but reflexive questions have been given their special force in consequence of the recognition of the central role played by language, theory, sign, and text. Our concepts are no longer regarded as transparent – either in reflecting the world or conveying ideas. As a result all our claims about language and the world – and implicitly all our claims in general – are reflexive in a manner which cannot be avoided. For to recognize the importance of language is to do so within language. To argue that the character of the world is in part due to the concepts employed, is to employ those concepts. To insist that we are confined by the limitations of our own problematic, is to be confined within those very limits.

Rooted in the modern concern with the sign, as language or theory, reflexivity has surfaced in divergent fields in superficially different guises. In factual disciplines such as science or history, anthropology or psychology, reflexive questions have been raised because the so-called 'facts' on which such disciplines are based are no longer uncontentious. Empirical observation is questioned on the grounds that it is theory dependent. Common sense is doubted on the grounds of cultural relativism. This questioning, however, has led to views which are unstable. Such claims as 'there are no facts', 'there are no lessons of history', 'there are no definitive answers or solutions', are all reflexively paradoxical. For, is it not a fact that 'there are no facts', and a lesson of history that 'there are no lessons of history', and a definitive answer that 'there are no definitive answers'? Often these reflexive problems are ignored, as if they were merely irritating details that could be forgotten about; on other occasions *ad hoc* means of escaping the paradox are hastily erected. Indeed, so long as an arena of certainty is retained the problems of reflexivity can remain at the level of entertaining, but essentially trivial, logical puzzles. Historically such certainty has been found in God, in phenomenological experience, in empirical observation, and in the beliefs of common sense. But today, because of the irreducibly textual character of our beliefs, all arenas of certainty are in question. Our 'certainties' are expressed through texts, through language, through sign systems, which are no longer seen to be neutral. It appears, therefore, that in principle there can be no arena of certainty.

Questions of reflexivity, in their current form, have not been restricted to the sphere of 'factual' disciplines. Writers, literary critics, artists, and film-makers, have in their own fields tried to express concerns raised by reflexivity. So the writer discusses the role of the author, the artist includes his own easel in the painting, the film-maker films the making of the film. Each of these moves attempts to situate the narrator within the narrative itself, as if to demonstrate its narrative form while at the same time seeking to escape that very narrative. In a certain sense such moves must fail, for the narrative is always merely a narrative and identifying it as such is no means to escape its character. Within each of these attempts, whether by Magritte or Godard, Calvino or Truffaut, we find an aporia which is opened up through reflexivity. We have for millennia, accepted the distinction between fact and fiction, reality and myth, truth and falsity. Reflexivity poses a threat to this distinction, and in doing so threatens facts, reality and truth, but so does it also threaten fiction, myth and falsity.

Nietzsche, Heidegger and Derrida do not figure in this book merely because they are concerned with reflexivity – it was not after all a new phenomenon – but because they take the destructive aspects of reflexivity to their limit. In consequence, they can be seen to open up the postmodern world – a world without certainties, a world without absolutes. This new impact of reflexivity is in part due to a critical shift of focus, from the individual subject to the text. Thus from Nietzsche to Derrida we see the subject – traditionally the focus of philosophical thought as the place of experience, morality, choice and will – gradually abandoned. The power of the destructive force thereby unleashed was such that they regarded all previous thought as having been placed in jeopardy.

The alternative modes of thought which these philosophers

10

propose both rely on, and incorporate, a reflexivity which is all-encompassing. As a result, perhaps, their claims are grand to the point of being outrageous. For Nietzsche, Heidegger and Derrida, do not merely seek to change our views, but propose a new mode of thought. They regard themselves as standing at the end of a 2000-year-old tradition whose errors they seek to expose; for Nietzsche, its Christianity; for Heidegger, its metaphysics; and for Derrida, its logocentrism. As the ruins of an era of thought, for us *the* era of thought, lie around them, the future is portrayed as so radical a break from the past that we can barely image what it may hold. Almost a century ago Nietzsche wrote: 'One calculates *time* from the *dies nefastus* ['unlucky day'] on which this fatality arose – from the *first* day of Christianity! – *Why not rather from its last? – From today?*'[1]* Eighty years later, Derrida is at times no more circumspect in his vision: 'The future can only be anticipated in the form of an absolute danger. It is that which breaks absolutely with constituted normality and can only be proclaimed, *presented*, as a sort of monstrosity.'[2]

Not surprisingly these apparently wild claims make some English-speaking philosophers feel uneasy, trained as they are in a tradition that admires the detailed and painstaking research of science. As a result such remarks are more likely to be interpreted as incipient megalomania than the product of a closely argued philosophy. For many, therefore, the writings of Nietzsche, Heidegger and Derrida illustrate the worst aspects of continental philosophy. Their work is seen to contain unsubstantiated claims, nonsensical statements, and speculative excess. Nor has the unease been limited to philosophers. Nietzsche has been portrayed as a pernicious, even evil, influence on the twentieth century. George Steiner does not exaggerate when he remarks that the impact of Heidegger's work has been regarded by some as 'nothing less than disastrous, both philosophically and politically'.[3] The writings of Nietzsche, Heidegger and Derrida, have generated emotions of such intensity, not simply because of their criticisms of the tradition, but on account of the fear of the alternative. For their writings have been associated with an attack on rationalism; and without the safety of rationalism, on which our tradition is in part built, what is there to constrain the excesses of power, caprice and prejudice? Some have therefore seen the 'irrationalism' of these

---

*Superior figures refer to the Notes section at the end of each chapter.

philosophers as not merely undermining, but actively dangerous. Their 'irrationalism' is not, however, adopted lightheartedly, but as a response to, and a product of, reflexivity.

The Great Enterprise

In the Anglo-Saxon world, philosophical criticisms of Nietzsche, Heidegger and Derrida have taken a number of different forms. In the 1930s, the logical positivist philosopher, Carnap, singled out Heidegger's remarks on Nothing to demonstrate the 'absurd pseudostatements'[4] that could result if we allowed the grammatical form of language to run away with us. In Nietzsche's case the points on which he has been praised are perhaps more significant than the criticisms, for it is the style of his prose, his poetic use of language and his command of metaphor, and not the force of his philosophical argument, that has found the most widespread recognition. While Derrida has been cited to illustrate the almost deliberate obscurantism and lack of clarity that is seen to pervade much of the continental tradition since Hegel.

Despite the great influence of Nietzsche, Heidegger and Derrida in fields as diverse as politics, literary criticism and theology, their writings have been largely ignored by analytic philosophers. Their work, with a few exceptions, has not been regarded as sufficiently rigorous to warrant inclusion in the corpus of true philosophy; its complexity and obscurity has in general been regarded as a lack of clarity, the contortions and evasions of their writing as evidence of its confusion. The paradoxical formulations which litter their writing are thus taken as serving to demonstrate the total failure of their approach, and as such are no more than a dire warning of where such views lead.

The dismissal of the works of these philosophers points to a fundamental dispute over the character and function of philosophy itself. The charge that Nietzsche, Heidegger and Derrida are not engaged in philosophy evidently seeks to reduce the weight we should attach to their conclusions. If we can regard their works as literature, or perhaps poetry, we do not have to dispute their conclusions and can content ourselves with commenting on the quality of the writing. Implicit in this view is the assumption that philosophy is something more than literature. Its claims are more substantial since they are the product of rigorous thought and analysis. But it is precisely this view that Nietzsche, Heidegger and Derrida call into question.

In order to indicate the nature of this disagreement we shall describe one, slightly caricatured, version of the role and function of philosophy. From this standpoint philosophy is seen to take part in the great enterprise of knowledge by setting aside all incidental and contextual detail, and concerning itself solely with the character of things in general. Human desires, the social and historical context and the constraints of our concepts are all hindrances to this project, but they can be overcome and do not jeopardize its possibility. This view does not imply that philosophy must provide a grand metaphysical picture of the world, but it must at least seek to articulate the ground, or the rules according to which we must operate. Since Kant, transcendental arguments have played an important role in this enterprise. These have attempted to show that certain concepts, principles or modes of justification are necessary in order for us to have experience at all. According to this view, whether philosophy provides a total account, in the manner of Plato, or whether it simply provides the framework, in the manner of Kant, it is engaged in the project of knowledge by which we move, painstakingly perhaps, towards a more complete understanding of the world.

Since the Enlightenment the achievements of science have provided the propaganda for this enterprise; for, more than being a mere philosophers' dream, it has been the dream of the European tradition. According to this account, through the diligent application of reason and empirical method we have gradually added to our fragments of knowledge. Philosophers, in overseeing these advances, must distinguish between those areas of which knowledge is possible and those which must remain unknown. In the first category are facts (the great enterprise consisting of the gradual acquisition of these facts), and in the second category are values. The value-laden must be carefully removed and isolated from the facts, for only uncontaminated, pure facts are allowed to acquire the character of knowledge.

In contrast, Nietzsche, Heidegger and Derrida do not regard philosophy as providing the foundation, the core of certainty, on which scientific knowledge claims can rest. Such a foundation is, they argue, illusory, as is the possibility of the project of knowledge that it seeks to underwrite. Nietzsche, Heidegger and Derrida are certainly not the only philosophers to question the foundational role of philosophy –

such views are widely held among contemporary English-speaking philosophers – but their abandonment of the great enterprise is linked to a wholesale attack on reason, empirical method, and the distinction between fact and value. These are very broad claims, but echoes can be found in the analytic tradition, such as Wittgenstein in his later writings, and the pragmatists Dewey and James.

The denial of the possibility of knowledge may seem a wild and anarchistic claim, but it is at first sight intelligible and *logically* unremarkable. But matters cannot be left there. This denial involves a reflexive problem, which appears trivial but which cannot be eradicated with the ease that one might expect: if it is not possible to provide knowledge, then how are we to regard the text of the philosopher that asserts this very point? Since it is evidently paradoxical to claim to know that knowledge is not possible, philosophers who have wished to make this type of claim have usually engaged in the more wide-ranging attempt to alter the nature of their text in order to avoid a self-contradictory stance. Despite the importance of this question, vital qualifications in the writings of Wittgenstein, James and Dewey which shift the character of their texts in response to this problem have often been ignored, and other philosophers have proceeded to use their arguments to derive fully fledged theories of meaning or truth of precisely the type that they have endeavoured to avoid. The texts of Nietzsche, Heidegger and Derrida are less capable of this misreading, for their texts are more systematically elusive: at times we are presented with a multiplicity of theories, at other times the theory once propounded is later denied.

The charge that the enterprise of knowledge must fail, and the assertion that a final account is impossible, have an impact on every field of 'knowledge', not least on philosophy, the role of which, in the provision of the foundations of knowledge, makes it particularly susceptible to these criticisms. It is not accidental, therefore, that philosophers who have held this view, from Wittgenstein to Nietzsche, have denied philosophy its traditional role – sometimes to the extent of almost denying it a role at all. For those who find some affinity with this point of view, and who wish to put an end to definitive theories, the concern with reflexivity is forced by what can seem an irritating afterthought, which is linked to the question of status that we have just raised. Is the argument that it is not possible to provide more than a provisional explanation of why we should hold a belief or act in a certain way, provisional as well? Is the denial of the possibility of a final account the final word? Nietzsche, Heidegger and Derrida begin their philosophy having already asked this question, a question which they demonstrate cannot be ignored, but which, one suspects, they can never answer – at least in a conventional sense – either.

The persistent puzzle

The intractability of the texts of Nietzsche, Heidegger and Derrida can to some extent be explained by the unfamiliarity of their concepts, but it is also the result of the themes which these philosophers address. Reflexivity is one of these central themes, and without a recognition of its role the texts are likely to appear unnecessarily convoluted and can seem to achieve little. Seen in the light of reflexivity, the works are given an internal rigour and coherence more commonly associated with analytic philosophy. The paradoxes which these philosophers seem to embrace can no longer be interpreted as poetic indulgence, perverse eccentricity, or empty mysticism, and may instead be seen as the inevitable product of their interpretation of the world. The evasive style and elusive character of their claims are thus a means of expression forced upon them, rather than a vacuous play with obscurity. One further factor which makes a reading of these philosophers difficult is that the concern with reflexivity, although pervasive, is largely implicit. This implicit character of reflexivity is not accidental, for to use a typically paradoxical Derridean description, if one could approach this central theme directly it would at once cease to be central, and would no longer have the character of a theme.

Reflexivity functions in the texts of Nietzsche, Heidegger and Derrida in two diverse ways: on the one hand it is a means of critique, a weapon to be used against the great enterprise of knowledge; on the other, it is a positive movement employed in the proposed alternative. The former technique is an instance of perhaps the most traditional philosophical manoeuvre – the demonstration of contradictions within the views of your opponent – and is certainly not unique to these philosophers. Hegel, for example, uses a reflexive argument of this type in his critique of Kant. Kant had argued that certain concepts were necessary in order for us to have knowledge. These concepts, or 'categories', could not be demonstrated in the same way that we might demonstrate Newton's laws of motion, but according to Kant they could be shown to be necessary if knowledge is to be possible. Hegel's argument was that Kant, in providing these conditions for knowledge, presents them as objects of knowledge themselves. This cannot be possible, however, because the form which thought must adopt cannot itself be expressed within thought, for that expression must itself be made in the context of those necessary forms.

This type of argument, which tries to show that the theory presented in a text itself reflexively denies the possibility of that theory, employs an extension of a minimal form of reflexivity which can apply to individual statements. Reflexivity in this limited sense is familiar to analytic philosophers and is associated with a set of logical puzzles, which we will examine in a moment. Nietzsche, Heidegger and Derrida were not concerned with analysing such logical conundrums and in so far as they remain merely puzzles, they are of more concern to the mathematician than to the philosopher. However a consideration of this minimal sense of reflexivity is required if we are to appreciate the widespread and all-encompassing use of reflexivity which all three of these philosophers employ.

Reflexivity in this most limited form is a term used to describe the self-referring character of a statement or group of statements. Some statements self-refer in an obvious and unexceptional way: 'This sentence contains five words.' However, from the liar paradox onwards it has been recognized that statements of this self-referential nature can generate paradoxes. The original version of the liar paradox appeared in the sixth century BC, when the Cretan prophet Epimenides allegedly observed that 'All Cretans are liars.' Since he was a Cretan this claim appears to deny itself. A more general form of this paradox is contained in the statement 'I am lying' – for if one is telling the truth the statement must be false, while if one is lying then the statement is true. Recent versions of the paradox have been considered in such statements as 'This sentence is false', but they serve merely to provide further examples of a claim that is falsified in the very statement of that claim.

It is evident that the paradox generated by these statements only occurs if the statement is deemed to reflexively include, or refer to, itself. If, in some way, the statement can escape this reflexive reference the paradox evaporates. For example, if Epimenides was not Cretan there is evidently no difficulty with the claim 'All Cretans are liars.'

Similarly, the reason that such paradoxes do not tend to arise in everyday conversation is that we assume, albeit implicitly, that the statement does not self-refer. Thus 'I am lying' will often be taken to mean that the person is lying in some respect which excludes his or her claim to be lying. Indeed, to insist upon strict self-reference can often appear irritatingly pedantic.

On encountering paradoxes of self-reference philosophers have in general followed this common-sense approach, and have attempted to remove such paradoxes by excluding from the reference of such claims the claim itself. In the case of a statement such as 'There is no truth', a paradox arises as soon as the self-referential character of the claim is recognized. If there is no truth, then it cannot be a truth that there is no truth. Thus if this claim is to be maintained a distinction has to be introduced so that 'There is no truth' refers to a limited region of statements, allowing the statement itself to be asserted as a truth. So long as the statement can belong to higher order, a meta-level, the self-reference can be avoided and the paradox evaporates.

This form of reflexive problem is less easily dispatched when the introduction of another level itself generates a further paradox. Suppose we wish to say of sentences at the meta-level that 'There is no truth.' To avoid paradox we would have to resort to a meta-meta-level. This would successfully avoid the paradox in this instance, but if we wish to claim that 'There is no truth' generally, we are left with an endless hierarchy of meta-levels. When Russell encountered a reflexive paradox in his attempt to found mathematics on logic, he developed this form of solution in his *Theory of Types*. Russell's problem was not that he wished, in the manner of a sceptic, to assert a reflexively paradoxical claim of the form 'There is no truth', but that he wished to ensure the exclusion of such paradoxes from his logic. In an attempt to achieve this Russell argued that the problem was one of illegitimate totalities. A totality for Russell was illegitimate when it involved all of a collection of which it was itself a part. As an example of the paradoxes generated by this error, Russell cited the following case. A barber in a small town shaves everyone in the town who does not shave themselves. The paradox is who shaves the barber? If he shaves himself, then he should not do so, for the barber only shaves those people in the village who do not shave themselves; while if he does not shave himself then he is, of course, one of those people who is not shaved by the barber. Russell's solution was to argue that a class must

17

belong to a higher logical type than the elements that belong to that class.

By this manoeuvre Russell hoped to eliminate such paradoxes from his logic. In the process, however, he was committed to a complex hierarchy of types. Within the aims of his enterprise few have regarded this as a satisfactory solution. It has seemed both *ad hoc* and over-complicated, as well as possibly having unwanted ontological implications. But even if such a move is successful in founding a paradox-free logic, it does not solve the problem for the person who wishes to make a claim which by intent includes the characteristic of being paradoxically self-referential. To return to the example of 'There is no truth', an endless hierarchy of levels might enable us to avoid paradox on any particular occasion but in the end there must be a level at which the claim 'There is no truth' no longer applies. It is evident that if the intention is to imply generally that there is no truth, the manoeuvre ceases to be satisfactory. If the claim merely concerns religious belief, or moral and aesthetic values, there would be no problem. It is only when the claim is extended to all areas that the paradox begins to appear unavoidable. Russell's move simply bans this type of all-embracing general claim – which is only acceptable if you are prepared to limit the claim in some way. Accepting the limitation is no minor affair, for it involves the implication that there is after all an arena of truth – and it is a denial of this very implication that is for Nietzsche, Heidegger and Derrida at the root of the claim in the first place.

It is at this point that philosophers have traditionally tended to conclude that a general claim of the form 'There is no truth' is untenable precisely because it is paradoxical. Instead of trying to retain the claim that 'There is no truth', or some similar paradoxical statement such as 'All is relative', we should abandon it and modify our views accordingly. Since reflexive paradoxes of this form are often overlooked by those who make such claims, it is often assumed that a mere demonstration of the reflexive paradox involved is sufficient to show the impossibility of the position. The demonstration of reflexivity in this form has been a familiar move against sceptics since the Greeks. If the sceptic claims that 'We cannot know anything', the counter has been to point out that even the sceptic claims to know something, namely that 'We cannot know anything'.

Apart from their use in philosophical argument reflexive paradoxes that grow out of this simple form can initially appear to have the

18

character of a mathematical teaser that can be put away into the almost harmless box of logical puzzles. Disturbingly however these reflexive paradoxes are found at the root of our most fundamental theories. For example, the two most prominent philosophies of science produced in this century both have a reflexively paradoxical starting point.

In the case of the logical positivists truth and meaningfulness were defined in terms of satisfying criteria derived from the scientific method. According to this view, 'only empirically verifiable statements are meaningful'. However, this statement is itself not empirically verifiable. Moreover the problem cannot be solved by tampering with the criteria involved in 'empirical verifiability', since any criterial definition of rational acceptability, in terms of institutionalized norms, will encounter the same problem. Unless this central principle of verifiability can avoid self-reference in some way it must be regarded as meaningless. The logical positivists conceded the point, and tried to rectify the situation by arguing that their criterion of meaningfulness was not a claim about the character of the world but only a proposal. By this manoeuvre they hoped to place the criterion in a different category and thus avoid reflexive paradox. However, in addition to being *ad hoc*, having removed the claim from the sphere of cognitively meaningful statements, it is difficult to see how it is possible to argue for it, as they clearly wished to do.

A more recent philosophy of science, associated with Kuhn and Feyerabend, faces a similar reflexive argument. Both of these philosophers have argued that science does not develop only by a process of rational justification. Feyerabend further argues that there is no such thing as final rational justification. Each culture, and each age, provides its own paradigms of rationality. The reflexive difficulty here is immediately apparent. How can Feyerabend argue his case, citing examples from the history of science, if his conclusion is that rational justification is not possible? Feyerabend can, of course, answer this question in its present rather trivial form: while final justifications may not be possible, interim justifications within a context could be retained. However, his denial of the supremacy of science, his assertion of the incommensurability of terms in a different culture or epoch, and his advocacy of theoretical anarchism, are not intended as interim moves. (If it is argued that these are interim claims, the claim that these claims are themselves interim cannot itself be regarded as interim without inducing a sense of vertigo that would

19

destroy all meaning.) The denial of the supremacy of science, however, implies the denial of the supremacy of his own theory as well. Thus Feyerabend's claim that there can be no criteria for overall rational acceptability appears reflexively undermining in a way that parallels the opposite claim made by the logical positivists that a set of criteria, which they had provided, must be satisfied in order for a statement to be deemed rationally acceptable.

Apart from the two theories of science already noted, the problems of reflexivity appear in many forms of relativism. The claim may take an historical form: 'our interpretation of society is a function of history'; or a social relativism of the type: 'our views are determined by our society and the place we take in that society'; or it may take a cultural or linguistic form; but in each of these cases to avert the potential paradox a meta-level must be introduced to enable self-reference to be avoided. These difficulties are often most evident in disciplines which are already of a meta-order nature. Thus the sociology of knowledge and theories of science are immediately faced with this problem for they are attempts to provide a theory (knowledge) about how theories are possible (how knowledge is possible). The means by which a new level is introduced to avoid self-reference risks appearing *ad hoc* if it merely excuses this particular theory without a satisfactorily general explanation. Mannheim, for example, having argued that truth is socially determined, allows his own theory to escape this description by introducing a meta-level of an intellectual élite who are able to break through social determination – an explanation which seems to amount to claiming that 'truth is relative for you but not for me'.

The move of avoiding self-reference by the provision of a meta-level inevitably reintroduces a realm of possible certainty which provides what may be called a ground, a foundation or an absolute. A theory which declares the importance of context is thus forced to find a means of escaping the limitations of that context. As a result the attack on the project of knowledge implicit in such a theory is radically diminished – a foundation and a certainty to our knowledge are after all possible. Previous arguments asserting the context-dependent character of our beliefs or our observations are no longer so threatening since the theory of that context-dependence turns out to be context-free. And if that theory is context-free then others can be also. The vision of a gradually expanding, properly grounded arena of knowledge remains intact.

20

For those who have recognized the potentially damaging effects of self-reference, but who have not been prepared to resort to the provision of a meta-level, we can discern two responses to the problems. The first of these approaches incorporates self-reference into the theory, so that this particular example of self-reference is itself an instance of a more general characteristic. Thus if it is argued that our theories are historically or culturally relative, this particular view should itself be predicted by the theory. Hegel and Marx can both be interpreted as engaging in a manoeuvre of this kind. Without this addition Marxism would appear to face a typically reflexive problem. If, as Marx argues, the views or ideology of individuals or classes are the product of their social and historical position, then this must also be true of Marx and his theory. If, as Hegel argues, history is the unfolding of Spirit, then the Phenomenology of Mind and the description of that unfolding must itself be part of the unfolding. In both cases the theory is itself seen as the product of the historical forces that it outlines. The theory thus accounts for its own existence. One may suspect, however, that in both cases the theory gives itself a privileged position by arguing that this theory is the theory which accompanies the culminating historical form. In Marx's case, it is not clear whether the theory of dialectical historical materialism based on a class analysis of society is, or is not, taken to be open to further modification in the light of altered historical and social circumstances; and if it is open to modification to what extent?[5] The two most common responses to this question have been to argue either that we have reached the final stage in society/thought and that therefore, unlike all previous theories, this theory has the character of a science; or, that although the theory is a product of its historical and social context, it can develop in the light of circumstance or practice. Despite the fact that the conclusions are provisional, therefore, they take part in a gradual movement towards a final, true, account – though this may never actually occur. The first of these explanations effectively introduces a meta-level; the second attempts what might be described as a dialectical solution, by incorporating the idea of change within the theory. Thus although a description of our context is itself determined by that context, an interaction between the theory and the context allows for a development in which the theory moves forward. Theory and context are thus interwoven in a dialectical relationship which is itself described by the theory. However, the suspicion must remain that either the theory of dialectics which describes this interweaving illegitimately excludes itself from the dialectical change that it describes, or, if it is capable of such change, it is no longer clear what the theory is asserting.

Another attempt to avoid paradoxes of self-reference has consisted of arguing that no general metaphysical claims are implied by any statement. Both pragmatists such as James and Dewey, and the later writings of Wittgenstein can be regarded as taking up this type of option. Although James and Dewey had things to say about truth, they did not intend these remarks to be taken as describing the essence of truth. Their remarks instead take place in the context of an attempt to do something, rather than an attempt to assert something. James may have said that the true is 'what is good in the way of belief' but this is not part of an attempt to provide an all-embracing theory of knowledge; rather it is an attempt to change the way we go about doing things. We use our theories to convince others, and to alter their actions. They are not part of a grand scheme to provide the final description of the world.

The later Wittgenstein provides a similar means of avoiding the paradoxical effects of reflexivity in his attempt to avoid any general theory of language, and to explicate philosophical problems by showing how language is in fact used. When challenged, the pragmatist or the Wittgensteinian can simply refuse to be drawn on the nature of their overall theory, and can instead respond with a reply specific to the issue in hand. Any account or theory proposed is merely given for a particular proposal and does not imply any overall general claim.[6] Their response is therefore not final, but part of a social interaction; one could say it is conversational.[7] The conversation can never be ended, for there is no definitive remark that would silence the topic for ever; but nevertheless some remarks are more effective than others. Because no claims are made that have an eternal all-embracing character the paradoxes previously associated with relativistic claims about truth are apparently avoided.

Reflexivity endorsed

Nietzsche, Heidegger and Derrida take up a radically different stance to any of the 'solutions' we have considered in relation to reflexivity, for they do not regard reflexivity as eradicable, or as requiring solution. They thus appear to endorse paradox. Their writings might therefore be readily dismissed, were it not for the accompanying claim that the paradox is unavoidable. In consequence, their writing tends to fall into two parts: first, the demonstration that the positions taken up by other philosophers are reflexively paradoxical, and second, the presentation of their own account. The demonstration of the reflexive contradictions inherent in the writings of others (in the writings of those who pursue the enterprise of knowledge), instead of leading to a demonstration of how such contradictions can be avoided, is used to argue that such inconsistency is inherent in all writings of the great enterprise. Each of these philosophers expresses this conclusion in a somewhat different form, but each is left with the dilemma of how to proceed if the tradition, which they all of necessity find as their context, is doomed to inconsistency.

It would, of course, be a mistake to consider that any of these philosophers provide an alternative system to replace the theories of previous philosophers; since they are challenging the view that a definitive theory is possible. Nevertheless, how can one write a philosophy, which is surely a theory of sorts, in a way which denies the possibility of theories, without falling into meaningless or unintelligible paradox? This question of how to write a text in the light of the implications of its own reflexivity is the central concern which all of their writings can be seen to address. It is, therefore, not a very effective criticism of these texts that they are paradoxical, for at one level they do not claim to be otherwise – indeed one might say that they insist upon it, and in doing so a challenge is made to the foundations, or, they would argue, the assumed foundations, of our tradition.

Since to follow the footsteps of these philosophers is to throw into question our fundamental assumptions, while at the same time to be unclear of what alternative is being proposed, we will wish to have some evidence that the inconsistencies in the enterprise of knowledge are in fact apparent, and furthermore cannot be avoided, before proceeding much farther. There is no shortage of such evidence in the texts of Nietzsche, Heidegger and Derrida; indeed, one of the ironies surrounding their writings is that although their texts can appear radically inconsistent – some would say incoherent – it is the charge of inconsistency that these philosophers maintain against the whole of the tradition. Much of Nietzsche's writing is devoted to a demonstration of the contradictions of other philosophers, and many of his books, such as *Twilight of the Idols* and *The Genealogy of Morals*, consist of little else. Only his book *Thus Spake Zarathustra*, written in an almost biblical style, could be said to be a positive expression of an alternative rather than a negative critique. Similarly, Derrida's work is dominated by a critique of previous thinkers. Indeed in his case the method of critique – deconstruction – appears at times to be elevated to the level of a positive 'theory' in its own right. With Heidegger, although his own theories are more apparent, much of his writing is devoted to a description of errors in the history of western thought. Fortunately, there are parallels among the concerns of English-speaking philosophers which will help to indicate why Nietzsche, Heidegger and Derrida regard the paradoxes of reflexivity as unavoidable, and the task of the great enterprise hopeless.

Language has perhaps been the dominant concern of twentieth-century philosophers. Shortly after the turn of the century the philosophy of logical analysis maintained the view that confusions in our use of language had been responsible for philosophical disputes throughout the ages and that a close attention to logical form would eliminate these issues once and for all. Although this view is no longer widely held, the supposition that a close attention to the workings of language is the means to pursue philosophical argument remains. A central character of the modern perspective has been the replacement of the traditional analysis of thought with an analysis of language. Nietzsche, Heidegger and Derrida share this concern with language and their view that reflexivity cannot be avoided is partly explicable in terms of their understanding of the role of language.

All three philosophers, Heidegger more clearly so towards the end of his career, adopt a position which at first sight appears to be a form of linguistic idealism. According to this view we find ourselves caught within the confines of language, and we are unable to step outside the limitations of the concepts within which we must operate. Language in this sense cannot be said to refer to reality, if by that we mean a given which lies outside language. 'Reality' is, after all, a word within language, as unable to escape the conceptual web as any other word. Thus Heidegger writes:

Human beings remain committed to and within the being of language, and can never step out of it and look at it from somewhere else. Thus we always see the nature of language only to the extent that language itself has us in view, has appropriated us to itself.[8]

Derrida, in describing what takes place when we read a text, says that we 'cannot legitimately transgress the text toward something other than it, toward a referent (a reality that is metaphysical, historical, psychobiographical etc.) . . . *There is nothing outside of the text*'.[9] Nietzsche takes up a similar position and at the same time indicates how we hide from the implications of this claim: '*We cease to think when we refuse to do so under the constraint of language*; we barely reach the doubt that sees this limitation as a limitation.'[10]

One of the senses in which Nietzsche and Derrida wish to make the reflexively paradoxical claim that 'there is no knowledge' is that, trapped within language, we cannot have any knowledge of the world beyond. There is no knowledge because we operate only in the theories and with the concepts of our language. We cannot know that something is the case because there is no way in which we are able to reach out to what is the case. But, as a saving move, we might argue that even if for the moment we accept that we are limited by language, we can define knowledge internally to language. Thereby knowledge might not have the same apparent force that it had previously, but we could have knowledge all the same. Why should it matter that the criteria for knowledge are ultimately linguistic? But, such a position cannot stand, and the argument against this being once again reflexive in nature. Its difficulty is indicated by Nietzsche's remark that 'we barely reach the doubt that sees this limitation as a limitation'.

The character of the problem can be seen by drawing a parallel with Wittgenstein. In the *Tractatus Logico-Philosophicus*, Wittgenstein tried to give an account of the relationship between language and the world. He employs a form of transcendental argument – the world and the way that language depicts the world must be of a certain form if thought (the picturing of propositions of language to ourselves), is to be possible at all. The character of language and the world must be such as to provide propositions with sense. Wittgenstein's account of the world does not follow so much from his view of language, therefore, but from the character that the world must have in order for language to be possible. The detailed form of his account is not for the moment important. One of his conclusions, however, is reminiscent of the remarks we have noted in Nietzsche, Heidegger and Derrida. For Wittgenstein is led to argue that 'The limits of my language mean the limits of my world'.[11] He is drawn to this conclusion because of the necessary character of the relationship between language and the world if there is to be sense. The reflexive problem that Wittgenstein then faces is that the theory that he outlines in the *Tractatus* attempts to describe the relationship between language and the world in a way that appears to transgress the limits of language which that theory itself claims cannot be transgressed. Wittgenstein concludes: 'The correct method in philosophy would really be the following: to say nothing except what can be said, i. e. propositions of natural science – i. e. something that has nothing to do with philosophy . . . '.[12] This sentence, in its attempt to state the correct method of philosophy, is itself reflexively unsettling, since it is evidently not a proposition of natural science. The same is true for the *Tractatus* taken as a whole – a philosophical theory about the character of language and the world which denies the possibility of such a theory. Wittgenstein is wholly aware of this reflexivity and as a result continues: 'My propositions serve as elucidations in the following way: anyone who understands me eventually recognizes them as nonsensical, when he has used them – as steps – to climb up beyond them'.[13] The theory has led us to the point where we must abandon the theory. Reflexivity, which in the case of Russell's paradoxes might have appeared as a mathematical teaser is here sufficient to cause Wittgenstein to place the whole status of his theory in question. One way of interpreting Wittgenstein's later writing is as an attempt to deal with this form of reflexivity by avoiding general philosophical claims altogether.

As Nietzsche implied, the reflexivity of 'the limits of language are the limits of my world' may not be immediately apparent. Let us consider this claim more closely. It appears to provide a description of a limitation in our understanding of the world. At first sight this would appear harmless enough, but it involves the same form of reflexivity as the logical positivist claim that 'only empirically verifiable sentences are meaningful'. Suppose for a moment we can view the situation from 'outside', from what we might call the 'God's eye view'. From this perspective we could observe people using language on the one hand, and the world on the other. Depending on what happened, we might then describe the experience of those using

26

language by saying that there was no more to their world than what they could describe in language. This God's eye-view is not, however, available for the language-users themselves precisely because their view is limited by language. Thus if Wittgenstein were correct in saying that 'the limits of my language are the limits of the world' he would not be able to say it in language, for to say it he would already have stepped outside language. Like the liar paradox, if it is true then it is false. Wittgenstein's distinction between saying and showing is an initial move in an attempt to explain such claims. However, the saying/showing distinction is itself part of the 'theory' proposed in the *Tractatus*, the concluding remarks of which seek to unsettle the whole edifice. It is therefore no more than a stopgap measure – since the distinction itself transgresses the limits of language.

The same form of paradox is generated by any overall claim about the world which incorporates within it the logical impossibility of its own verification. The paradoxical nature of these claims is more apparent if they are unpacked and simplified into the form 'the world is red and we have no means of determining that it is red' (e.g., the world is seen through language, and we have no means of determining that this is the case). Such assertions are paradoxical because they claim that one knows that the world is such and such while at the same time denying that this is possible. Hilary Putnam has recently tried to formalize this paradox using the example 'We are all brains in a vat.'[14] The paradox in this case arises in precisely the same way: if we really were brains in a vat we would be unable to know that we were brains in a vat, for to do so we could not be brains in a vat. Once again, like the liar paradox, 'we are all brains in a vat' is false if it is true. In these examples the reflexive paradox can be overlooked because we unwittingly, but illegitimately, move to the God's eye view from which there is no paradox.

Like Wittgenstein, therefore, Nietzsche, Heidegger and Derrida are led to an account of language which is reflexive and appears paradoxical. Unlike Wittgenstein they do not then abandon attempts to make general claims about the nature of language. Instead these claims are incorporated in a reflexive movement within their own theory. In Derrida's case this also involves demonstrating why reflexivity must arise in all texts, and why therefore the attempt to deny it, or avoid it, must fail.

We have concentrated on the reflexivity of certain claims about language, but this is only one aspect of the reflexivity found in the texts of Nietzsche, Heidegger and Derrida. The reflexive nature of these texts is often hidden, although it regularly surfaces in what appear as evident paradoxes. Claims such as 'what after all are man's truths? They are his irrefutable errors',[15] and 'Everything is false',[16] are thus not occasional aberrations but are part of an overall perspective in which reflexivity pervades the whole text. These particular dramatic examples, like the logical puzzles we considered earlier, are not in the end of great significance, for although they exhibit an elementary and immediately unsettling form of self-reference, the texts of Nietzsche, Heidegger and Derrida are reflexive throughout— the position of the theory or the text in relation to what it proclaims is always in question. Indeed, what it proclaims is also a function of that tension. Thus what is said in the text is always said in the light of the limitations of the text. The text is, therefore, never a given, a static object which can be examined as one would examine a statue. Instead there is a movement, a tension, between what can be said and what cannot be said. Thus descriptions are drawn, views held, and conclusions asserted, only later to be denied and cast aside. Nor is the denial to be seen as more valid than the assertion, for it is merely part of the continuing tension which pervades the text. No section of the text can therefore be taken at face value. No assertion is simply an assertion, for it carries within it the unsaid awareness that it cannot be asserted. In this sense reflexivity is no longer a form of self-reference, a paradoxical puzzle, or a philosophical argument, but an inescapable movement which is still present in the moments of apparent stillness. It is as if (to put it metaphorically!), we are caught in the metaphors of language and there is no way to halt their shifting character.

Although for notably different reasons, Nietzsche, Heidegger and Derrida, all find themselves compelled to argue from a position that involves a reflexive self-awareness which appears paradoxical. Most of their writing is therefore a response to this predicament rather than an argument for it. A simple reply to this whole predicament and one which will appeal to many analytic philosophers is to argue that to have arrived at this point is an indication of a fundamental error. So long as we regard the enterprise of knowledge, the dream of the Age of the Enlightenment, as intact, this argument will be a compelling one and the writings of Nietzsche, Heidegger and Derrida will remain of peripheral interest. If however, we are led to question the possibility of accomplishing such a project, for the reasons that they propose, or on account of Wittgensteinian, pragmatist, or other arguments, we will need in some form to come to terms with reflexivity, and in this respect the works of Nietzsche, Heidegger and Derrida must be of central concern.

The grand apocalyptic claims which assert the end of an era are therefore not so much the conclusion of their philosophies, but an initial rhetorical point from which these philosophers can begin. Because of the reflexivity of the resulting standpoint the denial of the great enterprise is also the beginning of a search to provide an alternative which is not simply another great project. In their attempts to provide such a perspective Nietzsche, Heidegger and Derrida propose radically new 'theories' of language, of Being and of thought. The quotation marks are necessary in order to indicate that these accounts are not to be treated as having the character of theories – as Nietzsche or Derrida might say, the privileged stories – that we sanctify in the pages of the encyclopedias of knowledge found in the great libraries of our culture.

Thus the antagonism that the writing of these philosophers has generated can be described as the inevitable response of those who find themselves defending the church of reason, and its hushed libraries, not from irrational hooligans but from treacherous high priests. But perhaps the real source of the antagonism is the fear that these priests will let in the hordes and the vandals. For are not these philosophers abandoning rationalism and with it the codes of behaviour which have constituted our precarious defences against the terror of unrestrained force? Adherents of this view will argue persuasively that it is not accidental that the names of Nietzsche and Heidegger have been linked with the Nazis. If there is no right in reason, or science, or thought, there is no wrong either. In fear, therefore, we cling to the Platonic and Kantian vision in the hope of suppressing the evil spirits that might otherwise overtake us.

It is Derrida's claim that we have always failed in this suppression. Our rationalism is beset with contradiction; the enterprise of knowledge, whose certainty was founded on the idea of immediacy, of presence, carried with it the impossibility of presence. While we may fear the abandonment of this project, and the accompanying comfort of certainty and promise of progress, if Derrida is right it is no solution to simply retreat from our modern awareness of context and reassert the

29

hope of the Enlightenment. So long as the security of the possibility of knowledge remains, the solution to questions of reflexivity will involve a step back towards this uncontentious certainty. From this perspective Nietzsche, Heidegger and Derrida will be interpreted as pursuing a contradictory, irrelevant and dangerous path. If, however, this comfortable option is no longer available, the writings of these philosophers give us an indication of the character of the world without the security of an all-embracing story. Such an undertaking is no small matter, for if 'Derrida is right' as we commented above, without the neatly defined pigeon-holes of logocentrism or rationalism it is far from clear, for reflexive reasons, what is involved in making such a claim. If 'the great project is over' it is not apparent how we can make this assertion. And if 'a new age is upon us', whether we view it as one free of constraint or one full of terror, is not the statement, and its categorical mode, sufficient to indicate that we remain within the old era? Nietzsche, Heidegger and Derrida may not provide us with solutions, but they do venture forth into this uncharted, and perhaps unchartable, reflexive territory. Regarding it as a risky, dangerous and possibly fruitless business, we may not wish to follow. Nietzsche, Heidegger and Derrida would, however, claim that we have no choice.

Notes

1 F. Nietzsche, *The Anti-Christ* (Penguin translation by R.J. Hollingdale) (Bucks 1968–74), sec. 62.
2 J. Derrida, *Of Grammatology*, translated by Gayati Spivak (Baltimore: Johns Hopkins University Press 1976), Exergue 5.
3 G. Steiner, *Heidegger* (Fontana 1978), edited by Frank Kermode, p.12.
4 R. Carnap, *The Overcoming Of Metaphysics Through Logical Analysis Of Language*, from *Heidegger and Modern Philosophy Critical Essays*, edited by Michael Murray (Yale University Press 1978), ch. 2.
5 cf. Z. Bauman, *Hermeneutics and Social Science* (Hutchinson 1978).
6 cf. Bambragh's essay in G. Vesey (ed.), *Understanding Wiggenstein* (Macmillan 1974).
7 cf. R. Rorty, 'Pragmatism, Relativism, Irrationalism', from R. Rorty *Consequences Of Pragmatism* (Harvester Press 1982).

8   M. Heidegger, *On The Way To Language*, translated by Peter D. Hertz (Harper and Row 1971), p. 134.
9   Derrida, *Of Grammatology*, p. 158.
10 F. Nietzsche, *The Will To Power*, translated by Walter Kauffman and J. R. Hollingdale (Vintage Books 1968), sec. 522.
11 L. Wittgenstein, *Tractatus Logico-Philosophicus*, translated by Pears and McGuiness (Routledge and Kegan Paul 1961), 5.6
12 ibid., 6.53.
13 ibid., 6.54.
14 cf. Hilary Putnam, *Reason, Truth and History* (Cambridge University Press 1981), ch. 1.
15 F. Nietzsche, *The Joyful Wisdom*, translated by Thomas Common (T. N. Foulis 1910), bk. 3, sec. 265.
16 Nietzsche, *The Will To Power*, sec. 602.

2

Nietzsche

Nietzsche is at the beginning of our story. Chronologically he was writing roughly a half-century before Heidegger, and almost a century before Derrida. Yet we shall also return to him at the end. For, it might be said, post-structuralists such as Derrida have not so much followed in Nietzsche's footsteps as rediscovered his philosophical stance – a stance that owes its character to an all-pervasive reflexivity.

The diversity of opinions expressed by Nietzsche in his own work has been matched by the diversity of interpretations of his writing by others. In the early decades of the twentieth century Nietzsche was widely read. In general, however, professional philosophers in the analytic school have had little time for his work. For example, Bertrand Russell's *History of Western Philosophy* (in George Steiner's phrase 'a vulgar but representative book'),[1] caricatures Nietzsche as the defender of evil who cannot be proved wrong but who is to be despised. Russell not only parades his moral distaste for Nietzsche's philosophy, but, more importantly, assumes that his writing is of a merely rhetorical nature and not worthy of rigorous philosophical examination. By way of explaining the fashion for Nietzsche, he is forced to say, 'It is undeniable that Nietzsche has had great influence, not among technical philosophers, but among people of literary and artistic culture.'[2]

In contrast to this dismissive view of Nietzsche's work a number of contemporary continental philosophers regard Nietzsche, in contrast to Marx, as being a seminal influence on the twentieth century. Deleuze sums up the present conventional wisdom in Parisian circles when he says, 'Probably most of us fix the dawn of our modern culture in the trinity of Nietzsche–Freud–Marx. Marx and Freud perhaps do represent the dawn of our culture, but Nietzsche is something entirely different the dawn of counter-culture.'[3] From this perspective Nietzsche is not merely a literary figure, or a great prose stylist, but a rigorous thinker. Indeed Deleuze uses phrases more commonly associated with analytic philosophy to describe Nietzsche's work:

Not only does all the rigour of his philosophy depend on it [accurate use of terminology], but it would be wrong to question its style and precision. In truth, Nietzsche employs very precise new terms for very precise new concepts.[4]

In what sense can Nietzsche's texts, full as they are of contradiction and stylistic flamboyance, be treated as rigorous? The answer to this question is to be found in the central role that reflexivity plays in his work. If the covert reflexive themes that underlie Nietzsche's writing are not recognized the text can appear incoherent and overblown. Reflexive concerns are partially responsible for some of the apparent eccentricities of Nietzsche's prose style, so that viewed in the light of reflexivity, Nietzsche can be seen to be thoroughly and even obsessively rigorous in his thought – to the point perhaps of both theoretical and practical self-destruction.

Before we look more closely at the function of reflexivity in Nietzsche's work a preliminary warning is necessary. Nietzsche, unlike Heidegger and Derrida, can appear relatively easy to comprehend at first glance. On further reading one is aware that this simplicity is illusory; yet the temptation remains of prematurely assuming an understanding of Nietzsche's text. Despite the apparent anarchy of Nietzsche's writing one cannot read any section of his work in isolation. As successive propagandists have found, one can cite Nietzsche in support of almost any cause so long as the quotations are chosen judiciously and one ignores all opposing arguments. One way to explain this would be to say that there are many complex levels of irony in Nietzsche's text so that claims cannot be taken at face value.

The problem of interpreting Nietzsche, however, is not simply a question of a careful reading, and the avoidance of assuming a conclusion before having read his other comments on the subject in question. For rooted in Nietzsche's philosophy is the implicit stance that there are no *final* conclusions; the text can never be fixed, and as a result it can never be deciphered either.

Relativism and reflexivity

Nietzsche's writing can be seen to fall into a destructive and a constructive mode. In both of these reflexivity plays an integral role. The destructive, negative aspect consists of an attack on the values and ideals – in Nietzsche's term 'idols' – of his time. The positive, constructive aspect consists in the replacement of these ideals with an alternative perspective. Nietzsche saw his own work in these terms, saying of his book *Beyond Good and Evil*, ' now that the yea- saying part of my life- task was accomplished there came the turn of the negative portion.'[5] Although Nietzsche's last books, following *Thus Spake Zarathustra*, are predominantly written from the negative aspect (' from that time onward, all my writings are so much bait'), it is the positive aspect which flows out of the negative. The passage from the negative to the positive is a critical one and is intimately linked with reflexivity.

Nietzsche's critique of the values of his time has numerous points of contact with the underlying pressures that have led to the erosion of the moral, aesthetic, and theological absolutes often seen as characteristic of the twentieth century. It is fifty years since the logical positivists attempted to remove moral judgements from the realm of fact- stating discourse. Today, G. E. Moore's assertion of a sphere of non- natural moral facts is likely to strike one as far- fetched, not on the logical positivist grounds that this metaphysical assumption is unverifiable, but on the grounds that morality is a function of social, historical, and cultural factors. Moral terms may have an objectively definable meaning, in any particular instance, but they do not refer to a universally acknowledged realm of moral facts. To this extent Nietzsche's attack on the moral dogmatism of his time has almost become a commonplace, and is initiated from a similar standpoint; ' an insight first formulated by me: that there are no moral facts whatever. Moral judgement has this in common with religious judgement, that it believes realities which do not exist'.[6]

Nietzsche predicted the collapse of absolute values, and described this as Nihilism. Today one would be more likely to use the terms relativism or perspectivism. Throughout this century there have been anthropologists and social scientists who have highlighted the cultural dependence of our values. In the mock biblical language of *Thus Spake Zarathustra* Nietzsche appears to make a similar point: 'Many lands saw Zarathustra, and many peoples: thus he discovered the good and the bad of many peoples . . . Much that passed for good with one people was regarded with scorn and contempt by another: thus I found it. Much I found here called bad, which was there decked with purple honours.'[7] Remarks that were, at the time, a radical criticism of prevailing views are now merely conventional. The following comment on aesthetics, for example, could almost have come from a current text-book 'the beautiful and the ugly are recognized as *relative* to our most fundamental values of preservation. It is senseless to want to posit anything as beautiful or ugly apart from this.'[8] However, despite its apparent similarity with a cultural, anthropological relativism, Nietzsche's relativism is more wide-ranging and thoroughgoing.

The anthropologists' assertion of cultural relativism has often been supported by the claim that individuals who from our perspective might be regarded as behaving badly, can be seen to be acting rationally given the constraints, beliefs, and circumstances under which they are operating. Typically, by using an example of what we regard as a grotesque rite of some distant tribe, the anthropologist is able to demonstrate that, far from being wrong, the activity has a beneficial effect on the individual and society.

Importantly, cultural relativists have for the most part been careful to limit their relativism to the values of society, thus leaving open the possibility of objective assessment through the observation of their physical world and behaviour patterns. If anthropologists extended their claim by saying that 'all is relative' it would no longer be clear how they might proceed. Putting aside for a moment the logical and epistemological problems posed by such a claim, an anthropologist making this assertion would appear to have deprived him or herself of access to the tribe in question, and thus of an understanding of its behaviour. For if 'everything is relative' any description of the tribe by the anthropologist must remain within the anthropologist's framework and thus outside the discourse and world of the tribe, the common ground on which observation could be based having been removed.

Replies can be made to this argument, but let it be sufficient to say that for reasons of this type, cultural relativism has usually been limited to the claim that only the values of a society are relative, leaving open the possibility of common 'facts'. Cultural relativism as a theory is therefore adopted as the result of empirical observation of many societies. The position is thus consistent and allows for further observation and the possibility that the view could be improved or even abandoned in the light of future research.

Although Nietzsche's relativism appears to be close to this form of cultural relativism, it is in fact of a different order. Nietzsche's relativism is not limited to values but includes what we regard as the arena of facts:

Against positivism, which halts at phenomena – 'there are only facts' – I would say: No, facts is precisely what there is not, only interpretations. We cannot establish any fact 'in itself': perhaps it is folly to want to do such a thing.[9]

Here, unlike the world portrayed by the cultural relativist, there is no true account; the world 'has no meaning behind it, but countless meanings – "Perspectivism" '. The central distinction is that, for the cultural relativist, although we may interpret the world differently according to our social context, there is a single world which we are all interpreting – the diversity of interpretations does not imply a diversity of worlds. For Nietzsche, however, there is no single, physical, reality beyond our interpretations: 'The perspective therefore decides the character of the "appearance"! As if a world would still remain over after one deducted the perspective! By doing that one would deduct relativity!'[10]

This extreme form of relativism has not been completely without supporters in the English-speaking world. Whorff at times seems to imply that different languages not only interpret the world in different ways, but generate different worlds: 'We cut up nature, organize it into concepts, and ascribe significances as we do, largely because we are parties to an agreement to organize it this way.'[11] Like many modern relativists, however, Whorff steps back from a full-blooded relativism and wishes to retain, at the very least, some sort of physical evidence – thus enabling him to avoid the problems associated with total relativism.

It is not surprising, therefore, that most care has been taken to guard against the ravages of relativism in the sphere of empirical observation and description. For this reason science, as the archetype of knowledge and with methodological links to empiricism, has been the last arena to be attacked on relativistic grounds. As we have noted, among English-speaking philosophers Feyerabend has recently taken up the most radical stance.

The reason for this special treatment of science is, of course, our little fairy-tale: if science has found a method that turns ideologically contaminated ideas into true and useful theories, then it is indeed not mere ideology, but an objective measure of all ideologies . . . But the fairy tale is false, as we have seen.[12]

Such a critique can be seen as the culmination of the attack on religious and moral absolutes half a century earlier. Indeed, Feyerabend employs the religious analogy in order to cast doubt on the special status claimed by science, 'that most recent, most aggressive, and most dogmatic religious institution'.[13] In this manner Feyerabend invites us to carry the relativistic critique of morals and religion through to science.

In making these claims Feyerabend finds himself closer to Nietzsche's view of science than any other analytic philosopher. For Nietzsche regarded science, like socialism, as an outpost of Christianity. Although his most profound and concerted criticism is directed at Christianity, the vestigial remains, Nietzsche argues, are seen to appear in science. The link that Nietzsche makes with Christianity is that science wishes to provide a total and absolute view of the world. The scientific God thus provides the framework of our understanding in the way that the Christian God had done previously. Science claims to have access to truths, and it is this metaphysical similarity that connects it to Christianity. Nietzsche denies science this special access and scoffs at its 'truths': 'All the presuppositions of mechanistic theory – matter, atom, gravity, pressure and stress – are not "facts-in-themselves" but interpretations with the aid of psychical fictions.'[14] Nietzsche's remarks would thus not seem out of place alongside those of Feyerabend.

It has been apparent to many that there is a problem with this standpoint. If, for example, we take a look at Feyerabend's claim: 'the fairy tale is false', he appears to have fallen into a circular, reflexive paradox. Feyerabend denies science has any special access to truth, not on the grounds of a superior alternative, but on the grounds that no special access is available. Are we to understand Feyerabend as saying that 'the fairy tale is false' *tout court*, or do we take him to be saying 'the fairy tale is false according to me'? If the former, Feyerabend is surely proposing another route to truth, another 'science' – his own – which has access to the facts in a way that he wishes to deny to the present archetype of knowledge. He would therefore appear to be forced into accepting the later formulation – 'the fairly tale is false according to me' – but in what sense is this claim any more than a whim? And if it is merely a whim surely there is no reason to take any more heed of it – other than perhaps to pacify any unfortunate overcome by this view, or, we should probably say, overcome by this feeling.

The cultural relativist limited relativism to the values of society with good cause for, as we have seen, total relativism falls into a reflexive problem reminiscent of the liar paradox. From Weber and Mannheim through to the plethora of linguistic, historical, sociological and anthropological relativisms prevalent today, consistency is retained by limiting the relativism in some way, so that the theory itself is able to escape its own critique. For it is only when relativism takes on an all-embracing, total character that it becomes reflexively paradoxical.

The conclusion that most analytic philosophers have therefore drawn from the reflexive paradoxes surrounding total relativism has been that limits must be imposed in order to retain consistency and intelligibility. In short, access to some form of objectivity must be left open. Hilary Putnam writes:

Like Sextus Empiricus, who eventually concluded that his own scepticism could not be expressed by a statement (because even the statement, 'I do not know' could not be one he *knew*), the modern relativist, were he consistent . . . should end by regarding his own utterances as mere expression of feeling. To say this is not to deny that we can rationally and correctly think that *some* of our beliefs are irrational. It is to say that there are limits to how far this insistence that we are all intellectually damned can go without becoming unintelligible.[15]

Analytic philosophers who have been aware of this problem may have differed over their formulation of the solution, but they have agreed on one thing: there must be a solution, for otherwise we risk meaninglessness.

In contrast to most analytic philosophers Nietzsche makes no attempt to limit his relativism. Not content with the claim that there is no truth, which is paradoxical enough, Nietzsche goes further to assert that truth is falsehood. At this point the analytic philosopher is likely to conclude that Nietzsche is engaged either in unintelligible nonsense, or poetic meanderings. How else are we to interpret such excesses as 'Everything is false! Everything is permitted!'?[16]

Nietzsche, a great scholar of ancient philosophy, would not have been unaware of arguments akin to those of Sextus Empiricus. Yet Nietzsche writes, 'Ultimate scepticism – But what after all are man's truths? They are his *irrefutable* errors.'[17] Nietzsche has not overlooked the problem of reflexivity, but instead of retreating from the paradox by asserting access to a sphere of objectivity, he endorses the reflexive movement allowing it to unsettle our most deep-rooted convictions. In associating Nietzsche with the logical conundrums of the modern relativist we should not be misled into thinking that this set of issues is the only or even central aspect of Nietzsche's concern with reflexivity; but it does provide a link to contemporary analytic concerns and as such is a useful initial indication of the implicit reflexive themes that permeate Nietzsche's philosophy.

Once Nietzsche's endorsement of the reflexive implications of his claims is recognized the obvious question is whether he avoids unintelligibility, and if he does, by what means. However, before we consider this question we should be aware of the reasons Nietzsche would give for not taking the simpler path of allowing some degree of objectivity, and thus avoiding the apparent chaos that he is forced to embrace.

There are two explanations that Nietzsche provides to indicate why he regarded the option of retaining objectivity in some form as impossible. The first is linked to his interpretation of the history of philosophy, and the second with the rise of nihilism. From the wisdom of the Presocratics Nietzsche saw the history of philosophy as the development of an error. The decline is seen to begin with Socrates and reaches its high-point in Kant. The error previous philosophers are said to have made is the imposition of a real world, which is then made more and more inaccessible. To say that Nietzsche refused to introduce an element of objectivity because he regarded the imposition of the real world to be an error would, of course, come close to being a tautology. What we really want to know is why Nietzsche regarded the imposition of the real world to be an error – it is not, after all, a common-sense position.

Post-Kant, Nietzsche was writing in a tradition in which immediate access to knowledge could not be assumed. In the *Critique of Pure Reason* Kant tried to determine the conditions under which knowledge was possible. His account begins with the independence of intuitions and concepts, the elements of sensibility and understanding. Kant argued that in order for there to be knowledge these two elements had to be combined: 'Thoughts without content are empty; intuitions without concepts are blind.'[18] Kant then proceeded in his Transcendental Deduction to derive the Categories – the elements of pure understanding – the essential concepts through which the world must be seen if knowledge is to be possible. Since Kant believed that he had demonstrated that these concepts were essential for there to be knowledge at all, he had apparently provided a solid foundation for our beliefs. In his criticism of Kant, Nietzsche displays little reverence, often referring to him as 'old Kant', and in *Twilight of the Idols* as 'that most deformed conceptual cripple there has ever been, the *great* Kant . . .'.[19] There is more to Nietzsche's attack, however, than mere invective. The argument he employs against Kant is a reflexive one: Kant provides us with a critique of knowledge, thus describing the means by which knowledge is possible. However, in order to achieve this, he has to use the very tools that he is describing. If the *Critique of Pure Reason* is to provide us with knowledge it must itself be the product of the process that Kant describes in the Transcendental Deduction. 'A critique of the faculty of knowledge is senseless: how should a tool be able to criticise itself when it can use only itself for the critique? It cannot even define itself!'[20] There is another related argument that Nietzsche levels at Kant: Kant poses the question 'How is knowledge possible?', but to ask this question is to assume that we already *know* that knowledge is possible. If we already know this, and recognize that we know, is not the remains of the *Critique of Pure Reason* an elaborate development of this unquestioned starting-point? Nietzsche therefore concludes 'if we do not know what knowledge is, we cannot possibly answer the question whether there is knowledge'.[21] Of Kant's starting-point he is simply sarcastic: 'What is knowledge? He "knows" it, that is heavenly!'

Nietzsche therefore regards the critical enterprise as doomed to failure. Instead of the question 'How is knowledge possible?', Nietzsche wants to ask 'Is knowledge a fact at all?' The error that Nietzsche thus perceives in the history of philosophy is the assumption of the possibility of knowledge. Furthermore, Nietzsche does not regard this error as innocent. The motive behind it is the attempt to ensure the continuance of old values. 'The legitimacy of belief in knowledge is always presupposed . . . . Here moral ontology is the dominant prejudice.' Inevitably, in the wake of Kant it was not possible for Nietzsche to return to the simple 'dogmatic' position of postulating immediate access to knowledge. Once Nietzsche had abandoned the critical method as a mistaken enterprise there was little alternative for him but to make the radical move of denying all knowledge. The majority of his comments on Kant are made in the light of this conclusion.

Kant can be interpreted as responding to this sort of attack by making the distinction between the phenomenal and noumenal world, providing us only with knowledge of the phenomenal world and not of the noumenal. Perhaps unfairly to Kant, Nietzsche translates these as the apparent world and the real world, and then proceeds to criticize Kant for making knowledge of the real world 'unattainable, undemonstrable, cannot be promised, but even when thought of a consolation, a duty, an imperative'.[22] There are, however, some similarities between Nietzsche's conclusions in relation to Kant and the predominant analytic response. Twentieth-century English-speaking philosophers have in general dismissed Kant's talk of a noumenal world while finding his Transcendental Deduction, as applied to the phenomenal world, worthy of modification. Nietzsche regarded positivism as an advance on Kant, seeing it as a retreat from the real world into the apparent world, or in Kantian terms, from the noumenal into the phenomenal. The point at which Nietzsche parts company with the standard analytic view – which he would see as the stage beyond positivism – is at the point of abandoning the real world for the apparent world, he denies the real world *and* the apparent world: 'We have abolished the real world: what world is left? The apparent world perhaps? . . . But no! with the real world we have also abolished the apparent world!'

We will later see the function that this conclusion plays in Nietzsche's metaphysics. For the moment we should note that Nietzsche was unable to delineate an area of which we are capable of knowledge because of his reflexive criticism of the *Critique of Pure Reason*. He was thus led to make the paradoxical claims that there is no real world and there is no knowledge. Because of this, the first explanation that Nietzsche gives us for not being able to make the obvious move, of asserting access to a sphere of objectivity, to avoid the paradox of such remarks as 'there are no eternal facts, just as there are no absolute truths',[23] is linked to his perception of the history of philosophy. His second explanation rests on the view that the rise of nihilism leads to its own disintegration. As with the previous argument, the case hangs on a reflexive point: in this instance Nietzsche argues that the values of Christianity undermine themselves. 'The end of Christianity – at the hands of its own morality (which is insuperable), finally turns against the Christian God himself.'[24] A similar case is made against science: 'the industry of its pursuit eventually leads to a certain self-annihilation, an antagonistic attitude towards itself – a sort of anti-scientificality'.

Nihilism is not an attitude of mind which we choose to take on, but a stance that is forced upon us by the logic of our prevailing values: 'For why has the advent of nihilism become *necessary*? Because the values we have had hitherto thus draw their final consequences.'[25] It is our belief in truth that finally undermines the entire edifice – for our assumption of the possibility of truth eventually forces us to recognize the truth that there is no truth; 'Among the forces cultivated by morality was truthfulness: this eventually turned against morality, discovered its teleology, its partial perspective . . . .'[26] Thus Nietzsche saw the demise of absolute values as an historical necessity bound by its internal logic. In the preface to the *Will to Power* he writes, 'What I relate is the history of the next two centuries. I describe what is coming, what can no longer come differently: *the advent of Nihilism*.'[27] Bound by our present values, we are forced to apply them until eventually they disintegrate. Applied to the modern relativist this argument would run: 'You may try to set up a sphere of allowable knowledge claims, but according to your own criteria these will prove to be false.' A possible reply might be to ask whether Nietzsche is here making an empirical or an a priori claim. If it is empirical we can attempt to show that Nietzsche is wrong – although, as previous comments have indicated, the history of this century would indicate that Nietzsche at least has a case. If it is an a priori claim, however, we can use Nietzsche's own weapon against him – how does he have access to this knowledge? Indeed, this is only a specific reformulation of our original question, 'How does Nietzsche avoid falling into unintelligibility?'

The Nietzschean story

So far we have witnessed some of the negative, destructive aspects of reflexivity as employed in Nietzsche's writings; reflexivity as a criticism of previous philosophers, and also as an argument aainst the orthodoxies of Christianity and science. In attempting to answer the central question of how Nietzsche avoids unintelligibility we will witness the positive role of reflexivity in his writings.

We can determine two elements in Nietzsche's response to this fundamental question: a reinterpretation of the role and function of language, and a replacement of what he regarded as the implicit metaphysics of western thought with a radically different alternative. Reflexivity is integrally involved in both of these moves, which are themselves, inevitably, closely linked. For, as with all of Nietzsche's writing, to understand one part is to understand all parts, including that which denies the possibility of understanding. However, in order to enter what at one point Nietzsche will term 'the dance', at another 'the last day', and at another 'the noontide', one must begin somewhere; so let us begin with language.

At the end of a century which has seen language become the central concern of philosophy, both for analytic and continental philosophers, there is a risk of reading Nietzsche in the light of modern debates. Nevertheless, although Nietzsche was writing at a time when the role of the thinking subject was still perhaps the dominant theme of philosophy, he was no longer in a milieu that assumed language to be transparent. (Once Kant had linked concepts with intuitions, experience could no longer be regarded as independent of the concepts by which it is described. Kant thus laid the ground for an increasing role for language.) However, in Nietzsche we see the clear expression of an outlook characteristic of our modern stance, namely the virtual elision of thought into language. In a modern form of Occam's razor, Nietzsche almost eliminated thought. Language, instead of representing thought, provided concepts directly. 'Every word immediately becomes a concept, inasmuch as it is not intended to serve as a reminder of the unique and wholly individualized experience to which it owes birth.'[28] This is not to imply that Nietzsche denied the existence of thought– seen as a great influence and precursor of Freud, he often described himself as 'the great psychologist' – but to indicate that the character of language was for him equatable with the character of thought. For Nietzsche, therefore, to speak about language is to speak about thought. This much is today almost uncontroversial. Nietzsche however makes a stronger claim. Language, in providing us with concepts, also provides us with reality. Thus to frame a new description is to create a new reality.

Unspeakably more depends upon *what things are called*, than on what they are. The reputation, the name and appearance, the importance, the usual measure and weight of things . . . have gradually, by the belief therein and its continuous growth from generation to generation, grown as it were on and into things and become their very body; the appearance at the very beginning becomes almost always the essence in the end . . . . It suffices to create new names and valuations and probabilities, in order in the long run to create new 'things'.[29]

But Nietzsche is not a linguistic idealist – as if language was reality and there was no reality without language – rather he takes up the position that we are unable to escape the constraints of language and thus have no alternative but to operate within language. Such a stance is not so dissimilar from the late Wittgenstein, although the manner in which Wittgenstein restricts himself to a discussion of the detailed workings of language is radically different from the apparently cavalier way in which Nietzsche discusses reality and metaphysics. However, at points, Nietzsche employs arguments reminiscent in form to those of Wittgenstein – philosophical mistakes are seen to flow from grammatical errors. For example, Nietzsche regarded the importance given to the individual subject by nineteenth-century philosophers as a result of taking language too literally.

We find ourselves in the midst of a rude fetishism when we call to mind the basic presuppositions of the metaphysics of language – which is to say, of reason. It is this which sees everywhere deed and doer; this which believes in will as cause in general; this which believes in the 'ego', in the ego as being, in the ego as substance . . . . Reason in language: oh what a deceitful old woman! I fear we are not getting rid of God because we still believe in grammar . . . .[30]

There is a reflexive problem in relation to this view of language – of which Nietzsche was aware. For if we are to say 'we are trapped within language and its concepts', that claim is itself of course part of language; we wish to express our 'trappedness' but we are unable to so do other than in the very concepts which trap us. The original thought therefore eludes us, for if we could express it we would not after all be trapped. The reflexive paradox faced by Sextus Empiricus has here returned in a new guise.

Nietzsche approaches this topic directly in *The Will to Power*:

44

We cease to think when we refuse to do so under the constraint of language; we barely reach the doubt that sees this limitation as a limitation. *Rational thought is interpretation according to a scheme that we cannot throw off.*[31]

We see here two ways in which Nietzsche tries to deal with the problem. The first is to speak rather poetically, to postpone actual reference to the issue in question – 'we barely reach the doubt that sees this limitation as a limitation'. This move as a response to reflexivity is not one that is actually typical of Nietzsche, and we will later see this as the Heideggerian move. The second, a more familiar Nietzschean move, is to incorporate the paradox, 'rational thought is interpretation according to a scheme that we cannot throw off'. We know what Nietzsche is wanting to say, but he has apparently fallen into the unintelligibility of the extreme relativist. If we are really unable to throw off the constraints, to say so is to remain within the constraints. Nietzsche has here simply formulated a more complex version of 'we are trapped', and once again the thought slips from our grasp and a certain giddiness sets in; for if we understand the claim that 'we cannot throw off' the constraints of language we must already have thrown them off.

Having merged language and thought, and having made language to a certain extent constitutive of reality – 'we read disharmonies and problems into things because we think *only* in the form of language' – Nietzsche has apparently only become more deeply embedded in the reflexive mire. The key move that he now makes is to deny any fixity of meaning. Nietzsche is not to be understood as making claims that are to stand as assertions of truth. The present form of the paradox thus disintegrates. We are no longer able to draw up the paradox because there are no statements which can form a paradoxical relationship with one another. We cannot generate a contradiction because in order to have a contradiction we must have something which can be contradicted in the first place. By denying fixity of meaning Nietzsche has removed that possibility. Thus in the example to which we have previously referred, Nietzsche is not to be regarded as claiming as a truth that ' "we cannot throw off" the constraints of language'. To state it therefore no longer involves a contradiction – for there is no fact, no truth, being asserted which can be contradicted. But, you may say, if Nietzsche is not making this claim, what is he wishing to say? If whenever one pins him down he replies, 'well, I didn't really mean it', our eventual frustration is likely to lead to an outright dismissal of everything that he says. Indeed, this is precisely the reaction that has typified analytic thought. As a first response in Nietzsche's defence it should be said that although Nietzsche denies truths he is not denying all meaning; truths for Nietzsche are solidified metaphors. It is as if Nietzsche is always writing metaphorically; 'what then is truth? A mobile army of metaphors, metonyms, and anthropomorphisms . . . truths are illusions which are worn out and without sensuous power . . . to be truthful means using the customary metaphors'.[32] Nor should we regard this as a new truth; it is but another metaphor, which takes its place in Nietzsche's work alongside other metaphors for truth such as 'woman', and 'the will to power'.

We would be greatly misguided if we were to assume that because Nietzsche abandons truth and the fixity of meaning, he thereby abandons assertion. Anyone who takes even the most cursory glance at Nietzsche's writing will be aware that it is littered with statements issued in the most dogmatic manner, and which at first sight will be taken as assertions of fact. This is, however, one of the most common misreadings of Nietzsche which his own style encourages. Nietzsche's philosophical stance might have led him to write in the convoluted self-denying mode of some of his present-day French followers. Instead he chooses to adopt a variety of linguistic ruses, the most prevalent of which is a declamatory, oratorical manner. Nietzsche's denial of the fixity of meaning leads him to provide us with a plenitude of overtly contradictory claims on almost every subject. These are not to be interpreted as oversights or a lack of consistency on his part, but as an outcome of his attitude to language.

It is Nietzsche's use of a whole range of rhetorical methods that has led to him being regarded as a great prose stylist. Indeed the first overall reviews of his work in the late 1880s were along these lines. Nietzsche does not, however, use style for merely literary effect – as if style was something added to an otherwise dull text to make it more lively. Instead he regards style as an essential aspect of all writing which, even if one wanted, cannot be eradicated. One form of his rhetoric, which should not be regarded as more important than the others, is to adopt the style of traditional philosophy. Books like *The Genealogy of Morals* which approximate most closely to this, tend to be the ones most commonly read by analytic philosophers. However, for Nietzsche these books are no closer to making claims of fact than his most allegorical and metaphorical writing in *Thus Spake Zarathustra*. Moreover, although the 'truths' of *Thus Spake Zarathustra* are expressed in the most poetic form, it is these that Nietzsche regarded as his highest achievement. Nor should we think that the metaphors within *Thus Spake Zarathustra* have a stable meaning. Just when we think we have understood them, Nietzsche turns them round and uses them with the opposite value. With Nietzsche we are always in danger of assuming that we have arrived.

Typical of the weaving and interweaving of metaphors is the following section from Zarathustra's song in chapter 32: 'And when once Life asked me: "Who is she then, this Wisdom?" – then said I eagerly "Ah, yes! Wisdom! One thirsteth for her and is not satisfied, one looketh through veils, one graspeth through nets".'[33] First, we should be aware that when Nietzsche asks the question 'Who is she then, this Wisdom?', as well as giving a reply, the text shows the answer in the form both of the question and its response, for the entirety of the work is in a sense a response to the question 'What is wisdom?'. Nietzsche's use of a dialogue that begins 'What is she then, this Wisdom?' is thus already part of his reply. Bearing in mind this overall consideration, we should note that the first specific image of wisdom we are given in this section is as a beyond through the masks of language – 'One thirsteth for her and is not satisfied, one looketh through veils . . . .' Nietzsche, however, continues:

Is she beautiful? What do I know! But the oldest carps are still lured by her. Changeable is she and wayward; often I have seen her bite her lip, and pass the comb against the grain of her hair. Perhaps she is wicked and false, and altogether a woman.

Here is a second image of wisdom, not merely veiled but having the character of change, of ineffability. Nietzsche is here using 'wicked', 'false', and 'woman' with positive value. But even this image is itself called into question as Nietzsche continues, ' . . . but when she speaketh ill of herself, just then doth she seduce most.' Nor does Nietzsche let it rest here, making the rhetorical move of allowing Life to reply:

'Of whom dost thou speak?' said she. 'Perhaps of me? And if thou wert right – is it proper to say that in such wise to my face! But now, pray, speak also of thy Wisdom!' Ah, and now has thou again opened thine eyes O beloved Life! And into the unfathomable have I again seemed to sink.

47

As we noted earlier, this whole section functions to show the character of wisdom as well as to state it. Furthermore this complex web of metaphors is but a song in a section of the allegory which is *Thus Spake Zarathustra*.

Lost in a sea of metaphor, with apparently nothing left to grab hold of, we may feel that we have fallen into chaos. But Nietzsche's intention is to say that there is nothing apart from the meaning generated in the moment of interpreting his words. This is as true for Nietzsche, the author, as it is for us, the readers. Nietzsche often uses the image of words dying on him, as if in the instant of their inception and creation there is something which ebbs away as they gather the character of facts. For this reason Nietzsche sees every sentence as created or forged, as if out of nothing. This thought often gives Nietzsche's writing an appearance of megalomania, for implicit is the thought that in the creation of the sentence is the reality. And yet, in trying to capture the moment of the creation with words, Nietzsche is always behind himself, for as the sentence takes on the character of a truth it ceases to 'fly' and becomes pedestrian and statue-like.

We immortalise what cannot live and fly much longer, things only which are exhausted and mellow! And it is only for your *afternoon*, you my written and painted thoughts, for which alone I have colours, many colours perhaps, many variegated softenings, and fifty yellows and browns and greens and reds; – but nobody will divine thereby how ye looked in your morning, you sudden sparks and marvels of my solitude, you, my old, beloved – *evil* thoughts![34]

While it is true that Nietzsche shifts the nature of the reflexive paradoxes by denying the fixity of meaning – since, we are unable to formulate strict logical paradoxes because we have nothing firm to hold on to; $A \wedge \sim A$ cannot be deduced there being no A that we can assert – the question one will nevertheless wish to raise is whether, in denying the discreteness of meaning, Nietzsche is thereby reduced to meaninglessness. Nietzsche's answer is categorical: it is only through a denial of the discreteness of meaning that we are able to create any new meaning at all.

There would, however, appear to be a problem with Nietzsche's attitude to language that has a formal structure similar to the one associated with total relativism. If all Nietzsche's writing is metaphorical, surely there is no limit to interpretation, and if there is no limit to interpretation is not the resulting whirlpool carastrophic?

Alternatively, if some aspects of Nietzsche's writing are not meta-phorical, then we do after all have a means of access to truths, in which case it seems unnecessary to resort to metaphor in the first instance. In order to follow Nietzsche's response to these points we need to move on to the second element, namely his metaphysics, in answer to the overall question we are considering of how Nietzsche attempts to avoid unintelligibility.

The key terms in Nietzsche's metaphysics are, as we can now predict, metaphorical – the Will to Power, the Eternal Return, and the Superman. Given Nietzsche's attitude to language, it would be absurd to say that these terms can be 'translated' into more traditional philosophical usage; nevertheless, within the rhetorical context of this book, we have no alternative but to attempt to do so.

We have seen that Nietzsche's perspectivism does not consist in saying that there are different versions of the same reality but in saying that there are only perspectives – there is no reality beyond the perspective. Nietzsche avoids an idealist position for it is the lack of a single, unified reality that he asserts. In its place he gives us a world of becoming; a world in which nothing is eternal, in which everything is becoming other than what it already is. It is thus in the sense of a world of perpetual change that Nietzsche refers to the world as false. For to be true, would be to be such-and-such forever. It is for this reason that the world is, almost above all, not true. For Nietzsche therefore the changing character of the world, and its falsehood, are two metaphors of the same image, 'The world . . . is "in flux", as something in a state of becoming, as a falsehood always changing but never getting near the truth: for there is no "truth".'[35]

Nietzsche is not however able to assert straightforwardly that 'the world is becoming', for to do so would be to impose a world with an eternal characteristic, with a truth, namely that of becoming. Nietzsche is therefore unable to have knowledge of the world– even in its character of becoming– other than through metaphors that create new perspectives, which are themselves false and have to be discarded only to be replaced by new metaphors. Another image that Nietzsche commonly uses, which we have already come across in his remarks on language, is that of veils and masks. But these images do not imply a truth behind the veil:

We no longer believe that truth remains truth when the veil is withdrawn from it: we have lived long enough to believe this. At present we regard it as a matter of

49

propriety not to be anxious either to see everything naked, or to be present at everything, or to understand and 'know' everything . . . . Perhaps truth is a woman who has reasons for not showing her reasons?[36]

Nietzsche thus avoids the logical paradox associated with 'there is no truth', but in doing so presents us with an ever-shifting ungraspable reality – and it cannot even be that, for to have described it thus is to have grasped it.

The Will to Power and the Eternal recurrence are both linked to this underlying metaphysics, and are Nietzsche's means of overcoming the abyss. Nietzsche uses the term 'Will to Power' in a variety of ways but a first approximation might be to say that the Will to Power is the force which tries to impose on the world of becoming some order, some understanding, some truth. The Will to Power is thus a creator of meaning, a creator of value in a world which would otherwise be unfathomable.

Will for the thinkableness of all being: thus do I call your will! . . . Your will and your valuations have ye put on the river of becoming; it betrayeth unto me an old Will to Power, what is believed by the people as good and evil.[37]

The Will to Power is thus seen as knowledge, as an overcoming of chaos, as the provision of fixity in a world of change, as a means of making existence possible.

One should not understand this compulsion to construct concepts, species, forms, purposes, laws . . . as if they enabled us to fix the *real world*; but as a compulsion to arrange a world for ourselves in which our existence is made possible . . . The world seems logical to us because we have made it logical.[38]

The Will to Power is not therefore a faculty of individuals but the means by which individuals are possible. The self is but another fiction. One can see in this Nietzschean argument a parallel with Kant, a form of transcendental deduction, which instead of generating the categories generates the Will to Power. If this is what Nietzsche is doing he has reintroduced objectivity by the back door.

All of this may seem rather distant from the sense of the Will to Power which is most commonly alluded to – that of a political power relationship as between master and slave. Nietzsche's vision of the Will to Power as knowledge is incorporated into the world of nature and society by regarding the world as the resultant of conflicting wills to power, all of which are desirous of imposing upon and overcoming that which is not itself. It is in this sphere that Nietzsche is most easily understood as propounding some theory of competing individuals. 'Wherever I found a living thing, there found I Will to Power; and even in the will of the servant found I the will to be master.'[39] This is however only a surface, though not an unimportant, effect of Nietzsche's more fundamental vision of the Will to Power as a provider and creator in a world of falsity. The Will to Power is thus the means by which truths are made possible; as a result one might say, the Will to Power is Nietzsche's truth

'Truth' is therefore not something there, that might be found or discovered – but something that must be created and that gives a name to a process, or rather to a will to overcome that has in itself no end. . . . It is a word for the 'Will to Power'.[40]

Nietzsche cannot escape reflexivity, however, nor, it should be said, is it clear that he wishes to do so. The Will to Power cannot simply be the provision of knowledge in a world of becoming; for it would then *be* something absolutely – and that is not possible in a world of becoming. Nietzsche, in talking about the 'Will to Power', must exhibit the Will to Power. In speaking of overcoming as a means to knowledge, he must overcome overcoming as the form of knowledge. In recognition of this Nietzsche shifts the nature of the Will to Power from a specific capacity to an everlasting surpassing of itself. Nietzsche cannot rest content with a formulation of the Will to Power as a surpassing, for he must surpass this formulation also. In response to this the Will to Power becomes an originating force but one which we cannot conceptualize. 'The world, as force, may not be thought of as unlimited for it *cannot* be so thought of; we forbid ourselves the concept of an infinite force as incompatible with the concept "force".'[41] Nietzsche seems here to have reduced, or from an alternative perspective we might say heightened, the Will to Power to a perpetual reflexive overturning of itself. At this point are we not once again in danger of losing all content? Is this not simply unintelligible?

We have so far examined only one aspect of the complex metaphor 'Will to Power', but in terms of this aspect the Eternal Recurrence can be seen as an attempt at a resolution of the reflexive circle. It is a response to the otherwise unfathomable abyss in which Nietzsche finds himself. The Eternal Recurrence is an apparently simple idea that some have interpreted as merely the assertion of the circularity of time. Nietzsche, however, regarded it as the culmination of his thought.

In a world of becoming Nietzsche has given us the Will to Power as the provider of being and fixity. But in order to create, it has to be possible for the thing that is created to be. Without the possibility of being the Will to Power would always fail. So, in the metaphor of the Eternal Recurrence, Nietzsche combines being with becoming. The world is a world of becoming, but each moment is held eternally, asserted eternally. Change is asserted forever, but so is stability. Contradiction and falsehood are written in to the character of the world. Through the Eternal Recurrence the world is once again given being, but a being that has no unitary character. Thus after the whole of Nietzsche's virulent attack on stability, and fixity, and in its place the assertion of ever new metaphors, he writes in the context of the Eternal Recurrence 'the world exists; it is not something that becomes, not something that passes away'.[42] But in case we should take this as a repudiation of previous thoughts, he continues 'Or rather; it becomes, it passes away, but it has never begun to become and it has never ceased from passing away– it maintains itself in both.' In this culminating part of Nietzsche's metaphysics the metaphors of the Will to Power and the Eternal Recurrence are found to be metaphors of the world, and since there is no alternative to metaphor they are the world – *'This world is the will to power – and nothing besides!'*[43] In the Eternal Recurrence Nietzsche thus seems to try and incorporate the reflexive circle in the character of the world.

We have not here attempted a detailed account of Nietzsche's metaphysics. Many aspects of the Will to Power and the Eternal Recurrence have inevitably been left out. However, the point to note is that the terms within Nietzsche's own story are involved in a similar reflexive movement to the one we previously observed in connection with his views on language. Nietzsche's metaphysical terminology can thus be seen to neutralize certain reflexive paradoxes only for the reflexive movement to reappear in another form. The very overcoming that is the Will to Power is in part shown by this self-destructive character of Nietzsche's own story, a self-destructive character that Nietzsche is not only conscious of but actively cultivates. To return to the terms with which we began, Nietzsche faces reflexive concerns that have parallels with modern relativism, but instead of stepping back, which he regards as impossible, he endorses paradox and incorporates reflexivity into his own writing as a source of regeneration and as a motivating force. Reflexivity is not then, for Nietzsche, a negative force that one strives to eradicate, but a positive force that provides the life-blood of the new by unsettling the dead, and the dying, concepts which surround us.

While we may appreciate how he has come to this standpoint, when faced with Nietzsche's mixture of assertion and uncertainty, dogmatism and diversity, we must still consider the question of intelligibility. Even if we accept Nietzsche's metaphysics, and it is far from clear what that would involve, in what way is this more than an incomprehensible fairy-tale? How else are we to interpret a philosopher who so thoroughly denies the possibility of final interpretation, whose retreat into metaphor seems to know no limit? 'Verily no cyclone or whirlwind is Zarathustra: and if he be a dancer, he is not at all a tarantula-dancer!'[44] Nietzsche always appears to take the path of most difficulty; instead of closing things off and providing solutions, the horizon is constantly widened. If one reads Nietzsche in the hope that eventually the mist will clear and the entire landscape be revealed, one will be disappointed. One might wish to say that Nietzsche's account of the world is similar – the mist will never clear, the landscape will never be revealed – if it were not for the fact that this account, by providing an overview, does precisely that which it denies as it lifts the mist and shows the landscape. On a number of occasions Nietzsche warns us of this ever-present desire to see a conclusion, to think that the text has been comprehended, so that it can now be placed on the shelf safely digested. In *Ecce Homo*, Nietzsche writes of *Thus Spake Zarathustra*:

Here there speaks no fanatic, here there is no 'preaching', here faith is not demanded . . . . With all this is Zarathustra not a *seducer*? . . . But what does he himself say when for the first time he again goes back into solitude? . . . I now go away alone, my disciples! You too now go away and be alone! So will I have it. Verily I beseech you; depart from me, and guard yourselves against Zarathustra! And better still be ashamed of him! Perhaps he had deceived you . . . . Ye venerate me; but what if your veneration should some day collapse? Take heed lest a statue crush you![45]

Nietzsche's writing is characteristic of those philosophers who have been concerned with reflexivity in that, from the outside, he seems to dig himself into a deeper and deeper pit as his stance becomes progressively more incomprehensible; yet within his own perspective each move and shift is a necessary one. This divergence perhaps gives some clue of the reason for the disregard of Nietzsche's work by many English-speaking philosophers. The Nietzschean project can only begin from a sceptical starting point that questions the 'fact' of knowledge. If instead one adopts the more common-sense position, that scepticism is perhaps an entertaining diversion but essentially something to be refuted, the purpose of Nietzsche's writing becomes unclear, and the paradoxical excesses seem unnecessary. From the standpoint of common-sense we know the world before philosophical reflection begins; it is just a question of proving how it is that knowledge is possible. As we have seen, Nietzsche, for historical and possibly temperamental reasons, starts from the opposing point of view and ends up denying the possibility of knowledge altogether.

From one perspective, therefore, Nietzsche can appear self-indulgent and unthinking; as one of his biographers writes, 'it is tempting to explain the piled-up complexities of his writing very simply. His endless vanity made him reject everything anyone else had proposed. But to contradict everybody is to contradict yourself'.[46] Alternatively, we may doubt whether he is successful in his project, but we cannot question the validity of the attempt, or the subtlety and sophistication of his philosophy.

Nietzsche was not the first philosopher to be aware of reflexivity and incorporate it in some form, but he was the first to endorse and use its propelling force throughout his work: in Nietzsche there is no hiding place from reflexivity, no point of certainty, no final ground on which to rest. ' "Everything is subjective" you say; but even this is interpretation. The "subject" is not something given, it is something added and invented and projected behind what there is . . . .'[47] But this implies that something after all is doing the interpretation, you retort. But Nietzsche has always made the reflexive move; indeed he has usually made two or three. He continues: 'Finally is it necessary to posit an interpreter behind interpretation? Even this is interpretation, hypothesis.' And we might add for him – and this also. With Nietzsche, for the first time, reflexivity moves to the centre of the philosophical stage.

Notes

1 G. Steiner, *Heidegger* (Fontana 1978), edited by Frank Kermode, p. 11.

2 B. Russell, *A History Of Western Philosophy* (George Allen and Unwin 1946), p. 794.

3 G. Deleuze, *Nomad Thought*, from *The New Nietzsche*, edited by D. B. Allison, (Delta 1977), p. 142.

4 G. Deleuze, *Active and Reactive*, from *The New Nietzsche*, p. 89.

5 F. Nietzsche, *Ecce Homo*, translated by Anthony M. Ludovici (George Allen and Unwin 1911), p. 114.

6 F. Nietzsche, *Twilight Of The Idols*, Penguin translation by R. J. Hollingdale (Bucks 1968–74), p. 55.

7 F. Nietzsche, *Thus Spake Zarathustra*, translated by Thomas Common (T. N. Foulis 1909), pp. 65–6.

8 F. Nietzsche, *The Will To Power*, translated by Walter Kauffmann and J. R. Hollingdale (Vintage Books 1968), sec. 804.

9 ibid., sec. 481.

10 ibid., sec. 567.

11 S. Whorf, *Language, Thought and Reality*, edited and with an introduction by John B. Carroll (Massachusetts Institute of Technology 1956), p. 213.

12 P. Feyerabend, *Against Method* (Verso Edition 1978), p. 302.

13 ibid., p. 295.

14 Nietzsche, *The Will To Power*, sec. 689.

14 H. Putnam, *Reason, Truth and History* (Cambridge University Press 1981), pp. 162–3.

16 Nietzsche, *The Will To Power*, sec. 602.

17 F. Nietzsche, *The Joyful Wisdom*, translated by Thomas Common (T. N. Foulis 1910), bk 3, sec. 265.

18 I. Kant, *The Critique Of Pure Reason*, translated by Norman Kemp Smith (Macmillan and Co. 1929), p. 93.

19 Nietzsche, *Twilight Of The Idols*, translated by R. J. Hollingdale (Penguin 1966), p. 66.

20 Nietzsche, *The Will To Power*, sec. 486.

21 ibid., sec. 530.

22 Nietzsche, *Twilight Of The Idols*, p. 40.

23 F. Nietzsche, *Human All Too Human*, translated by Helen Zimon (T. N. Foulis 1911), p. 11.

24 Nietzsche, *The Will To Power*, p. 7.
25 ibid., preface sec. 4, p. 4.
26 ibid., sec. 5, p. 10.
27 ibid., preface sec. 2, p. 3.
28 F. Nietzsche, *On Truth and Lie in the Extra Moral Sense*, in *The Complete Works of Friedrich Nietzsche* edited by O. Levy (New York 1964), vol. 2, p. 174.
29 Nietzsche, *The Joyful Wisdom*, bk 2, sec. 58, p. 97.
30 Nietzsche, *Twilight Of The Idols*, sec. on Reason in Philosophy, p. 38.
31 Nietzsche, *The Will To Power*, sec. 522.
32 Nietzsche, *On Truth and Lie in the Extra Moral Sense*, NWIII, ii, pp. 374–5, TF180.
33 Nietzsche, *Thus Spake Zarathustra*, sec. 32, pp. 128–9.
34 Nietzsche, *Beyond Good and Evil*, sec. 296.
35 Nietzsche, *The Will To Power*, sec. 616.
36 Nietzsche, *The Joyful Wisdom*, preface sec. 4.
37 Nietzsche, *Thus Spake Zarathustra*, sec. 34, p. 134.
38 Nietzsche, *The Will To Power*, sec. 521, p. 282.
39 Nietzsche, *Thus Spake Zarathustra*, sec. 34.
40 Nietzsche, *The Will To Power*, sec. 552.
41 ibid., sec. 1062.
42 ibid., sec. 1066.
43 ibid., sec. 1067.
44 Nietzsche, *Thus Spake Zarathustra*, sec. 29.
45 F. Nietzsche, *Ecce Homo*, preface sec. 4, pp. 4–5; and *Thus Spake Zarathustra*, sec. 22, p. 90.
46 C. Brinton, *Nietzsche* (Harper and Row 1965), p. 75.
47 Nietzsche, *The Will To Power*, sec. 481, p. 267.

Further reading

The work Nietzsche regarded as his most profound, *Thus Spake Zarathustra*, is also his most elusive, and is not to be advised as a starting-point. It is probably best to begin with those works that are closest to English-speaking philosophy – *Beyond Good and Evil* or *The Genealogy of Morals*. The most recent translations by Walter Kaufmann, sometimes in collaboration with R. J. Hollingdale, have corrected inaccuracies in the original translations in the series *The Complete Works of Friedrich Nietzsche* edited by Dr Oscar Levy, but sometimes this is at the expense of the rhetorical force of the prose, and for this reason it is on occasion worth going back to the old translations. A short summary of Nietzsche's perspective is to be found in the final section of his own autobiography *Ecce Homo* (*Why I am Destiny*).

In France and Germany a number of the major philosophers of this century have written books on Nietzsche – Heidegger, Jaspers, Derrida, Deleuze. In general these are not useful introductions to Nietzsche's work, and tend to stand as primary works in their own right. However, Karl Jaspers, *Nietzsche: An introduction to the understanding of his philosophical activity*, tr. Wallraff and Schmitz (Gateway 1979), does approach the status of a commentary, though it is hardly an introduction.

As far as the secondary literature is concerned, a substantial number of the books in English adopt a biographical approach and, with a few notable exceptions, should be treated with caution as an indication of his philosophical position. For those interested in Nietzsche's life, F. A. Lea's, *The Tragic Philosopher* (Methuen 1957), and Hollingdale's *Nietzsche* (Routledge and Kegan Paul 1965) are to be recommended. Of the works that address themselves to Nietzsche's philosophical thought, the most widely available are those by Arthur C. Danto, *Nietzsche as philosopher* (Columbia Univ. Press 1965), Walter Kaufmann, *Nietzsche: Philosopher, Psychologist, Antichrist* (Princeton 1950), and J. P. Stern, *Nietzsche* (Fontana Modern Masters 1978). The most interesting collection of essays is to be found in *The New Nietzsche* edited by D. B. Allison (New York: Delta 1977). There is also a worthwhile collection edited by Robert Salmon, *Nietzsche: A collection of critical essays* (Anchor Books 1973), which includes articles across a wide spectrum and gives an indication of Nietzsche's extensive influence – it also contains a useful bibliography of works in English. Another collection of essays, *Nietzsche: Imagery and Thought*, edited by Malcolm Pasley (Methuen 1978), addresses itself to the divide between literature and philosophy, in so far as Nietzsche can both be seen as a poet and as a philosopher. For those interested in a deconstruction approach, De Man's essays on Nietzsche in *Allegories of Reading* are to be highly recommended.

3

Heidegger

The history of philosophy is the history of a mistake. It is the history of the forgetting of the question of Being. With the exception of some of the earliest writings of Greek philosophy, all other philosophers have covered up the issue of Being and have become lost in the mechanical workings of logic. However, beneath the empty juggling of their concepts and categories the hidden question of Being lurks and exerts its own demands on their texts. Thus although the tradition of philosophy is the history of a mistake it is an inevitable mistake that is brought about by man's relationship to Being. It is the question of Being and the nature of man's relationship to Being that is the true subject of philosophy and to which we must now turn, abandoning all that has come before.

Such a straightforward description might begin a summary of Heidegger's philosophy. It is, however, misleading, because it gives the impression that Heidegger is a philosopher of the old style, with a complete theory of history and truth, who wishes to replace the errors of the past with his own correct philosophical outlook; and it omits almost all that is of importance in Heidegger's work. Despite appearances, Heidegger does not attempt to provide us with an account of the history of Being, nor does he try to describe the nature of Being. It is even questionable whether Being is the subject of his contemplation, at least in the normal sense of 'subject'. We can say all of this and yet still accept the summary with which we began. It will be apparent therefore that one must approach Heidegger's thought with caution.

Heidegger's reading of Nietzsche gives an indication of his orientation and why our original summary was insufficient. At first sight Heidegger appears to have little in common with Nietzsche. In contrast to Nietzsche's virtuoso style and rhetorical excess, Heidegger's writing is dense; some would say impenetrable. While Nietzsche adopts a form of theoretical anarchism in response to his avoidance of system, Heidegger, in his monumental work *Being and Time*, apparently erects a grand metaphysical system. Furthermore, the subject matter of Nietzsche's writings ranges widely, while Heidegger has been regarded as having devoted the whole of his life to the contemplation of one topic – that of Being. Despite these differences, Heidegger regarded Nietzsche as the philosopher most worthy of attention (with the sole exception perhaps of the ancient philosopher Parmenides).

Nietzsche, as we have seen, used reflexivity in his writing both as a mechanism for destruction and as a force to be incorporated in the presentation of his own 'theory'. Heidegger is not unaware of these strategies. He applauds and develops Nietzsche's radical critique of previous thinking, accepting the Nietzschean view that the rationality characteristic of the 'last man' will reflexively destroy itself: 'in this species of last man, therefore, reason – the forming of representational ideas – will inevitably perish in a peculiar way, and, as it were, become self-ensnarled'.[1] More clearly than Nietzsche he argues that it is the representational character of reason that is the cause of its reflexive destruction.

This well made-up and well staged manner of forming ideas, of representation, with its constantly more refined mechanism, dissimulates and blocks from view what really is. And this dissimulation and blocking is not just incidental, but is done on the principle of a way of forming ideas whose rule is all-pervading. This type of dissimulating ideas is always supported by sound common sense. . . . Faced with this dissimulating type of representational ideas, thinking finds itself in a contradictory position. This Nietzsche saw clearly. On the one hand, the common ideas and views must be shouted at when they want to set themselves up as the judges of thought, so that men will wake up. On the other hand, thinking can never tell its thoughts by shouting.[2]

Heidegger therefore endorses Nietzsche's view that our present mode of thinking must destroy itself because of its reflexive contradictions. In addition he recognizes that this standpoint poses its own problems – 'thinking finds itself in a contradictory position'. Thinking cannot tell its thoughts by shouting, because to shout is to rely on the present mode of thought. If one is to approach a new mode of thought more stealth is required. Heidegger himself cannot therefore be interpreted as writing within the representational mode of thinking that

59

characterizes common sense. And it is here that we find the first reason for our unhappiness with the initial summary we gave of Heidegger's position. If Heidegger is critical of previous philosophers for adhering to the tradition of representational thinking, it would evidently be a mistake to read his own claims and assertions in this way.

Heidegger is sometimes critical of Nietzsche, more so in his writings before the Second World War, because he regarded Nietzsche as still caught within the tradition of metaphysics. As a result Heidegger often refers to him as the last metaphysician of the West. This critique, which due to his shifting perspective Heidegger is later careful to modify, is a reflexive one, arguing that Nietzsche's philosophy fails by its own criteria. Heidegger's argument centres around Nietzsche's notion of revenge: 'the will's aversion to time and its "It was" '.[3] According to Nietzsche, the Superman must overcome the desire to avoid transience, and is delivered from revenge by saying 'yes' to time. It is Heidegger's claim that Nietzsche himself succumbs to this revenge when at the end-point of his metaphysics he describes the Will to Power: 'to impress the character of being upon becoming — that is the highest will to power'.[4] Heidegger writes: 'is there not here a trace of revenge? A desire to end the transience of becoming?'[5] Thus Nietzsche is seen to be caught by revenge himself, unable to assert becoming but instead wishing to reduce it to being. One may suspect that Nietzsche is not so easily trapped, and indeed Heidegger seems to adopt this view in his later writings on Nietzsche. For the moment it is not important whether we accept this interpretation, because it demonstrates that Heidegger wishes to carry through the Nietzschean critique of metaphysics and is aware of the reflexive difficulties encountered in attempting to do so – since he uses this critique against Nietzsche himself. A further reason to hold our initial summary in abeyance, therefore, is that it implies a metaphysical system. Since Heidegger attacks Nietzsche, the most dissimulating of philosophers, for being metaphysical, it would be ridiculous to interpret Heidegger's own writing as an attempt to erect such an edifice.

We can see, therefore, that although different in many respects, Heidegger and Nietzsche adopt a similar outlook on fundamental issues. Like Nietzsche, Heidegger does not aim to provide any final answers, or to provide a complete, total account. Also, like Nietzsche, his philosophical writing does not assert a position but allows for movement within the text. This movement is not only encouraged but is essential to the task in hand. Such similarities are in part the product of Nietzsche's and Heidegger's awareness of the importance of reflexivity. As with Nietzsche, therefore, it is difficult to approach Heidegger's thought, for, written with an awareness of reflexivity, the texts are reticent about the very subject of which they wish to speak. For example, one aspect of reflexivity found in Heidegger is the 'hermeneutic circle'. Heidegger uses this term in his early writings to describe their method and structure. However, in the 1950s, in response to the question 'How would you present the hermeneutic circle today?' Heidegger writes, 'I would avoid a presentation as resolutely as I would avoid speaking *about* language.'[6] Certainly, if Heidegger is so determined to evade an account of his position it would be rash of us not to be wary in our attempt to make explicit that which he leaves unsaid.

The Heideggerian project

We can easily list the sort of things that Heidegger appears to be talking about – Being, thinking, language, questioning – but if he is not wishing to provide us with the truth, at least in the conventional sense, how are we to understand what he has written? If he is not attempting to present a metaphysical system, if he is not trying to provide an overall account, and if he is not wishing to write within the tradition of representation, what is his goal? One way of describing it might be as follows: Heidegger accepts the Nietzschean critique of previous philosophers, and extends this to the rationality of common sense which he regards as internally flawed; he is, however, not able simply to escape this rationality for he finds himself embedded in it. Although he uses a number of strategies by which he moves towards escape, the escape, on account of its own reflexivity, can never finally take place. Heidegger is thus always on the way to an escape. The form that this path takes is extremely varied, and develops from the hermeneutics of Being and Time to the more mystical approach of his later writing.

Heidegger, as we have noted, has been described as having devoted his life to the consideration of one topic. This central source of Heidegger's thought has been named Being, the being of Being, and the Being of beings. To name it with apparent simplicity, however, is to give the false impression that here we are to be engaged in the consideration of something which can be observed and described. Thus while it is true that Heidegger's writing, from the dense analytical detail of *Being and Time* to the poetic and mystical writing of later works, is in a certain sense concerned with the same topic, it is also one that goes by many names. This topic is indicated in a quotation Heidegger takes from Nietzsche in the lecture series 'What is called thinking'. It is the last sentence from Nietzsche's 'auto-biography', written in his student days, which reflects on the loss of childhood:

Thus man grows out of everything that once embraced him; he has no need to break the shackles – they fall away unforeseen, when a god bids them; and where is the ring that in the end still encircles him? Is it the world? Is it God?[7]

The difficulty we have in trying to define or describe the subject to which Heidegger addresses himself is due in part to the extent to which reflexivity is embedded in Heidegger's thought. When Heidegger speaks of 'Being' our inclination is to want to know precisely what he means. However the meaning of Being is systematically elusive:

'Being' proves to be totally indeterminate and at the same time highly determinate. . . . We have this contradiction: determinate, wholly indeterminate being. If we decline to delude ourselves, and if we have a moment's time to spare amid all the activities and diversions of the day, we find ourselves standing in the very middle of this contradiction.[8]

There are times when we are tempted to think that Being is almost defined as that which is elusive and ineffable. 'Being is not God and not a foundtion for or final abyss of the world . . . . Being is nearest to man. But this nearness is furthest from him.'[9] Any account or description of this central topic will be seen to undermine itself and appear in the process to disintegrate.

Heidegger's account of Being is thus immediately involved in a reflexive circle. Any description of Being must fail since it is that which necessarily eludes our mode of thought – and even this negative description of Being, as that which cannot be described, must be equally unsettled by its own reflexive self-denial. Heidegger's account of the philosophical tradition involves a similar reflexivity. Heidegger has concerned himself with philosophy from its origins – observable in the remaining fragments of Greek pre-Socratic writing – to the ontological categories of the medieval schoolmen, the metaphysics of Leibniz and Kant, and the terminus provided by Nietzsche. The summary with which this chapter began attempted to paraphrase the history Heidegger gives of this tradition as the history of the forgetting of the question of Being. Heidegger's relationship to the tradition, however, is not simply that of an impartial observer, for Heidegger is always reflexively aware that he is also part of the tradition; the forces that have operated in the work of previous philosophers, which he is apparently describing, must also apply in his case.

The question 'How does it stand with Being?' must itself remain within the history of Being if it is, in turn, to unfold and preserve its own historical import. In pursuing it we, in turn, shall hold to the discourse of Being.[10]

This implies that if, as Heidegger argues, Being has necessarily become hidden from view, then it must remain hidden from Heidegger as well. This recognition not only forces Heidegger to examine the function of his attempted interpretation of the tradition but also to require a method by which he can proceed in his own writing. Heidegger thus wishes to show up the constraints of the tradition while finding himself entwined in it.

The reflexive problems associated with this historical self-awareness are by no means specific to Heidegger and form a central strand of concern from Hegel through to the recent writing of Foucault, Habermas and Gadamer. An analysis of the tradition is used to uncover its prejudices. In Heidegger's case this involves demonstrating that the history of ontology is the surface effect of the structure of our being, of Dasein. However the task cannot be merely one of presenting an accurate account of the history of ideas; for the prejudices that one uncovers as necessary to the tradition are inevitably present in one's own analysis – precisely because they are necessary to the tradition. Indeed the prejudice that prejudices should be uncovered is central to the whole Western philosophical tradition. Thus, in 'uncovering' the tradition's prejudices one is in part merely reproducing them.[11] As a result the relationship with one's own text, as well as the texts of others, itself becomes complex.

In his early work Heidegger describes his method as being

hermeneutical. The question of interpretation with which herme-neutics is concerned, inevitably involves an understanding and an interpretation of one's own text. Gadamer, in his essay on Heidegger, sees in this particular form of the reflexive problem the central motor of the Heideggerian project. 'The recognition that all understanding inevitably involves some prejudice gives the hermeneutical problem its real thrust.'[12] This recognition provides the force and direction of the hermeneutic enterprise because if 'all understanding involves some prejudice', so does that understanding itself. If prejudice is inevitable one cannot eradicate it by uncovering all examples of prejudice, for that uncovery will itself be part of a new prejudice.

It is not surprising therefore that some have seen in Heidegger's position a straightforward circularity: he has to rely on the tradition and its categories of thought in order to criticize that tradition. Richard Rorty argues:

Heidegger wants to have it both ways, as did Kierkegaard in his day. Both need to invoke the tradition to identify what it is that has been wrongly approached, or has veiled itself. But both need to repudiate the tradition utterly in order to say what they want to say.[13]

There can be little doubt that Heidegger does find himself in the position of wishing to criticize the tradition that he is necessarily trapped in, but in his response he does not try to tell us what has been wrong with the tradition – at least in the sense of naming and describing the culprit. Were he to do so he would indeed have fallen into a contradiction. Heidegger, rather than viewing reflexivity as a paradox that is to be avoided, uses reflexivity as a positive means to escape from the tradition.

However, if Heidegger believes in his critique of the tradition, should he not simply abandon philosophy, or at least his metaphysical speculation, as Dewey and Wittgenstein can be interpreted as having done? This is, however, precisely what Heidegger urges us not to do, since he would regard this as the nihilistic culmination of the metaphysical tradition itself. Heidegger thus finds himself in the position of the philosopher described by Nietzsche: an ass that can neither carry its burden nor throw it off. As with Nietzsche, seen from the outside, Heidegger's thought is strewn with obscurities and paradoxes. But internally it can be interpreted as an attempt to come to terms with the reflexive abyss that threatens when one adopts the view that the philosophical tradition obscures and limits – since any attempt to move beyond it necessarily finds itself expressed in the terms, and context, of that very tradition. The reflexive abyss, instead of being viewed as destructive, is thus seen as the unsettling mechanism that enables us to approach that which must remain elusive.

Heidegger's analysis of the tradition is therefore less to do with providing an overall account of philosophical history and more a question of using historical analysis as a means of opening up his own predicament. Although his examination of the writing of other philosophers can appear as an attempt to uncover the final meaning of particular texts, a Heideggerian interpretation does not try passively to exhibit the original text. In the *Introduction to Metaphysics* Heidegger describes this process:

If we content ourselves with what the poem directly says, the interpretation is at an end. Actually it has just begun. The actual interpretation must show what does not stand in the words and is nevertheless said. To accomplish this the exegete must use violence.[14]

There are those who have understandably seen this as a means for Heidegger to reinterpret the philosophical tradition as he wishes, and undeniably there are times when Heidegger runs the risk of attracting this criticism. The function of his interpretations, however, runs parallel to his overall philosophical project, not by preparing a monolithic historical perspective on which his theory could be based, but as a means of opening up, and moving away from, the tradition in which we find ourselves. Hence his comments on interpreting Nietzsche:

To encounter Nietzsche's thinking at all, we must first find it. Only when we have succeeded in finding it may we try to lose again what that thinking has thought. And this, to lose, is harder than to find.[15]

Heidegger's examination of the tradition in order to open up his own predicament is not limited to analysing the works of other philosophers – perhaps his most central means of excavating the tradition is through etymology. In a parallel way to his examination of texts, by seeking the original meaning of a term Heidegger will often give the impression that he is thereby uncovering the true sense of the word. However it will already be apparent that Heidegger cannot be interpreted as seeking to provide us with a definitive account of the truth in any straightforward sense. The main function of his etymological analysis is therefore to shake our reliance on immediately available concepts, and breathe life into what have become empty categories. Etymology is thus a means of escape from the vacuousness of contemporary language. Our everyday language is seen by Heidegger as a spent weapon: 'Language in general is worn out and used up . . . . Everyone speaks and writes in language without hindrance and above all *without danger*.'[16] We have, as it were, forgotten the meaning of language. 'Everyday language is a forgotten and therefore used-up poem, from which there hardly resounds a call any longer.'[17] Etymology does not therefore provide a correct version of the meaning of the term, but is employed by Heidegger to unsettle the husks of meaning that surround us. Particularly in his earlier writing, it is one of the primary means by which Heidegger seeks to move out beyond the tradition.

The apparent certainty of knowledge is thus regarded by Heidegger as something to be overcome, rather than extended, if philosophy is to take place. Philosophy does not therefore have the character of the knowledge claims found in an encyclopaedia. In this basic stance Heidegger follows Nietzsche in arguing that philosophy cannot be a listing of truths. The truths of philosophy remain open and are never concluded. 'Philosophical questions are never dealt with as though we might some day cast them aside.'[18]

So far, we have seen the reflexivity of Heidegger's thought in relation to his interpretation of Being and the history of philosophy. These are both related to his fundamental philosophical stance which is one of questioning. Heidegger is not a philosopher who is seeking to provide us with answers. Instead he wishes to ask questions. In order to be able to ask a question, in this Heideggerian sense, we must have moved away from the certainty that Heidegger regarded as pervading the tradition of western philosophy. His account of Being and of the tradition of philosophy is thus an attempt to move towards a position where it is possible to question. And it is here, in Heidegger's understanding of the general nature of the philosophical project, that the reflexive character of that project is most apparent.

One of Heidegger's early formulations of the most fundamental question was 'Why is there something rather than nothing?'. The particular content of the question is , however, despite appearances, not of great significance. For if we could ask the question simply by uttering the words, there would be no reason why we could not also provide an answer. The point of the question is in its form rather than its specific content. 'To state the interrogative sentence . . . is not yet to question. . . . The interrogative sentence is not the question and not the questioning.'[19] The point of asking the question is thus to discover questioning, and the question chosen is not chosen because it is *the* question, but because it forces us to move towards this fundamental attitude. 'Really to ask the question signifies: a daring attempt to fathom this unfathomable question by disclosing what it summons us to ask, to push our questioning to the very end. Where such an attempt occurs there is philosophy.' In choosing the question 'Why is there something rather than nothing?' Heidegger hopes to unsettle our normal understanding of a question as a query with a discrete goal and thereby open up a wholly new region of concern. 'It is this questioning that moves us into the open, provided that in questioning it transform itself (which all true questioning does) and cast a new space over everything and into everything.'[20] Since the question is designed to challenge by questioning rather than by asking this particular question, it comes as no surprise that during his life Heidegger formulated a number of distinct and different questions all of which he regarded as fundamental: What is called thinking? What is this, this philosophy? How does it stand with Being?

Central to all Heidegger's questions is that they question themselves; and Heidegger, by attempting to ask these questions, is attempting to ask the question that underlies any particular question. The question that underlies all questions is a reflexive self-questioning.

This question 'why' is incommensurable with any other. It encounters the search for its own why. At first sight, the question 'why the why?' looks like a frivolous repetition ad infinitum of the same interrogative formulation, like an empty and unwarranted brooding over words. Yes, beyond a doubt, that is how it looks. The question is only whether we wish to be taken in by this superficial look and so regard the whole matter as settled, or whether we are capable of finding a significant event in this recoil of the question 'why' upon itself.[21]

Moreover, Heidegger does not perceive this question as arising rather irritatingly in a few abstruse areas of thought, but as being present everywhere if only we could uncover it. Thus Heidegger is not bringing our attention to a tedious logical conundrum, which we might solve in the manner of a crossword puzzle, but instead through this reflexive questioning he wishes to indicate an arena which has remained hidden (although trapped within our present framework even the indicating must remain partially hidden).

> Our question is the *question* of all authentic questions, i.e. of all self-questioning questions, and whether consciously or not it is necessarily implicit in every question . . . . It can never be objectively determined whether anyone, whether we, really ask this question, that is whether we make the leap, or never get beyond a verbal formula.[22]

An overlooking of the reflexive self-questioning of Heidegger's questions, and indeed of his whole work, thus removes the central purpose of the questions, and of his writing generally. It is in the light of this self-questioning that Heidegger is led to deny the possibility of describing the purpose or object of philosophy:

> There is no way of determining once and for all what the task of philosophy is, and accordingly what must be expected of it. Every stage and every beginning of its development bears within it its own law. All that can be said is what philosophy cannot be and cannot accomplish.[23]

It will now be apparent why an attempt to describe Heidegger's purpose and the object of his work is beset with a fundamental difficulty, for at the root of the Heideggerian project is the view that the purpose and object of philosophy must remain obscure – and this is, of course, just as true of his own writing. We may say, as we have done, that Heidegger's aim is to question. As it stands, this appears similar in character to the common perception of philosophy. However, if we knew what questioning consisted of, there would be no need to seek to question. Heidegger's questioning thus involves the question of what it is to question. Yet in this unsettling return of the question upon itself Heidegger catches sight of the nature of questioning. As the question returns it makes that which appeared clear appear elusive, and in that elusiveness there is an indication of what questioning involves. The indication must, however, always recede, for as soon as it reaches the point of an understanding, it has lost the character of questioning. Heidegger is thus always *on the way* to being able to question; yet it is never actually possible to arrive. Reflexivity is at once the reason that the arrival is not possible and the destabilizing source of unsettlement which provides the way. The reflexive character of Heidegger's work can therefore either be regarded negatively as a flaw which reduces the material to vacuity, or as the positive core which provides the motor, and characterizes the goal, of his writing.

Being and time

While there is a unity to the Heideggerian project, his approach varies significantly from his monumental early work, *Being and Time* (1926), through to his writings after the war. In retrospect Heidegger viewed *Being and Time* as an essential first step, but a step which, although necessary, was mistaken. For this reason he was able to say 'Only by way of what Heidegger I has thought does one gain access to what-is-thought by Heidegger II',[24] without contradicting his remark that 'the fundamental flaw of the book *Being and Time* is perhaps that I ventured forth too far too early'.[25] Therefore despite Heidegger's criticism of *Being and Time* it is only in the light of this highly detailed and analytical work that his later writings can be interpreted as anything other than empty mysticism.

It has been said that *Being and Time* was published in order that Heidegger could be elected to the chair of philosophy at Freiburg. This might explain why only the first two divisions of the first part of the work appeared. The third division and the whole of the second part were never completed, although the areas to be covered in these sections have to a degree been examined in other works. Although unfinished, *Being and Time* provides Heidegger with a framework that he is able to draw on for the rest of his life. We cannot attempt to paraphrase the work here, or perhaps anywhere – in principle – but we shall attempt to throw light on the central role of reflexivity in two areas: first, the method of *Being and Time*, and second, the structure of the theory presented.

There are two adjectives that Heidegger uses to describe his method in *Being and Time* – hermeneutic, and phenomenological. For Heidegger, phenomenology does not refer to the science of phenomena but rather to a way of going about philosophy.

Our treatise does not subscribe to a 'standpoint' or represent any special 'direction'; for phenomenology is nothing of either sort, nor can it become so as long as it understands itself. The expression 'phenomenology' signifies primarily a *methodological conception* . . . rooted in the way we come to terms with things themselves.[26]

Heidegger's method plays a rather different and grander role than one would normally expect; his method is not a means of achieving a conclusion, in the way that Cartesian doubt can be regarded as a means to certainty. Heidegger is advocating a method of proceeding not as a halfway house on the road to proclaiming a position but as an end in itself. ' "Phenomenology" neither designates the object of its researches, nor characterizes the subject-matter thus comprised. The word merely informs us of the "*how*" with which *what* is to be treated in this science gets exhibited and handled.'[27]

The formal definition that Heidegger gives us of 'phenomenology' is not terribly helpful: 'to let that which shows itself be seen from itself in the very way in which it shows itself from itself'.[28] Characteristically opaque and apparently circular, this formulation, typical of Heidegger's style as a whole, is only of much use when we are already wholly immersed in the Heideggerian system. By 'phenomenon' Heidegger means 'that which shows itself in itself' [29] but this is not to describe things of the character of Kant's phenomena, 'entities which are accessible through the empirical "intuition" ', but such things as space and time– for Kant the forms of intuition. The phenomena that Heidegger is investigating are therefore precisely those 'things', like space and time, which do not show themselves in a normal sense at all.

What is it that phenomenology is to 'let us see'? What is it that must be called a 'phenomenon' in a distinctive sense? . . . Manifestly, it is something that proximally and for the most part does *not* show itself at all: it is something that lies *hidden*.[30]

This hiddenness is central to phenomenology, and that which is covered up and hidden Heidegger calls Being. 'Yet that which remains *hidden* in an egregious sense, or which relapses and gets *covered up* again, or which shows itself only "*in disguise*", is not just this entity or that, but rather the *Being* of entities . . . .'[31] Phenomenology therefore becomes the uncovering of that which is hidden. Since if it were uncovered it would no longer be that which was hidden, the reflexive paradox in the enterprise is evident from the beginning. The vortex that is opened up by what Heidegger calls the 'cardinal problem' – the question of the meaning of being– becomes apparent when we realize that if the meaning of Being is hidden from us we cannot hope to answer the question, and if it is not hidden from us it is no longer referring to that which Heidegger wishes it to refer to. Since the subject matter of phenomenology cannot be described, for it is that which is hidden, phenomenology itself cannot be reduced to a simple technique. Thus a general characterization of phenomenology and hermeneutics must remain at root ineffable. We may, however, gain a preliminary idea of what is meant by these terms by looking at the particular form of method that Heidegger employs in *Being and Time*.

The task which *Being and Time* sets itself is to formulate the question of the meaning of Being. In response to this, Heidegger distinguishes between Being and beings. The way he attempts to move towards articulating the central question of Being is to analyse the Being of man, which Heidegger calls Dasein. Heidegger chooses to analyse Dasein rather than any other type of being, such as tables or animals or mountains, because the character of the Being of Dasein is special, and furthermore leads to the uncovery of the question of the meaning of Being in general. For Heidegger argues that what distinguishes the Being of man from the Being of all other beings is that Dasein is that being for whom the question of its own Being is central to its Being. For Heidegger, therefore, the nature of our Being is to be reflexively concerned with the nature of that Being. In this way Heidegger both separates Dasein from all other beings, and places reflexivity at the centre of its Being. Thus while a stone has Being, it is only Dasein that is concerned with its own Being. For us, Heidegger argues, existence is not an unquestioned simplicity but is an existence which owes the character of its existence to its own concern with that existence. Furthermore, since the character of Dasein is to be concerned with its own Being, a preliminary understanding of Being in general must be available to us. Thus Heidegger argues that an analysis of Dasein is not prior on account of it being *our* existence, which would turn the enterprise into an anthropological exercise, but on account of the special character of Dasein's Being which implicitly involves an understanding of Being as a whole. Dasein is therefore unique among entities in the world and the character of this uniqueness enables us to approach the queston of Being. Through the reflexivity of Dasein's Being we can approach the question of Being as a whole.

Dasein does not fit into either of the traditional philosophical categories of 'subject' and 'object': certainly it is just as mistaken to regard *Being and Time* as an analysis of the subject as it is to regard it as an anthropological examination of the form of man's existence. 'Subject and Object do not coincide with Dasein and the world.'[32] Dasein is an 'object', as an entity within the world, and thus for Heidegger 'ontic' and a 'subject' concerned with its own Being and with Being as a whole, and thus 'ontological'. Early in *Being and Time* Heidegger provides us with a preliminary description of Dasein:

. . . an entity which does not just occur among other entities. Rather it is ontically distinguished by the fact that, in its very Being, that Being is an *issue* for it. But in that case, this is a constitutive state of Dasein's Being, and this implies that Dasein, in its Being, has a relationship towards that Being – a relationship which itself is one of Being. And this means further that there is some way in which Dasein understands itself in its Being, and that to some degree it does so explicitly. It is peculiar to this entity that with and through its Being, this Being is disclosed to it. *Understanding of Being is itself a definite characteristic of Dasein's Being.*[33]

While the special, reflexive, characteristics of Dasein enable Heidegger to claim that he is moving towards the meaning of Being, it is also these characteristics that generate successive paradoxes.

We have outlined the generally reflexive character of Heidegger's stance with regard to phenomenology and the character of Dasein; in the method of *Being and Time* this reflexivity emerges in two specific ways. First, we are engaged in an analysis of Dasein in an attempt to approach the meaning of Being, but this analysis can only proceed if in some sense we already know the answers. Indeed Heidegger in his preliminary description of Dasein already ensures that this is possible by including this as a characteristic of Dasein – hence the sentence in the earlier quotation 'there is some way in which Dasein understands itself in its Being, and that to some degree it does so explicitly'. As *Being and Time* unfolds, this characteristic of Dasein appears in different guises. One of Heidegger's favourite phrases is 'always already', and this, applied to the Being of Dasein, is often a way of describing this implicit circularity. Thus Dasein can be said to have always already understood the meaning of Being, for this is a condition for the possibility of Dasein as a being for whom Being is an issue for it.

[the world] has already been disclosed beforehand . . . . The world is therefore something 'wherein' Dasein as an entity already *was*, and if in any manner it explicitly comes away from anything, it can never do more than come back to the world.[34]

Thus paradoxically Dasein always already understands the meaning of Being even though we are never able to give an account of the meaning of Being.

A further aspect of reflexivity as it applies to the method of *Being and Time* is that Heidegger's own interpretation of Dasein must itself be a product of Being. Thus Heidegger will argue that the moves philosophers have made in attempting to provide an ontology are themselves the inevitable and necessary product of the underlying character of Being.

If, then, the answer to the question of Being is to provide clues for our research, it cannot be adequate until it brings us the insight that the specific kind of Being of ontology hitherto, and the vicissitudes of its inquiries, its findings, and its failures, have been necessitated in the very character of Dasein.[35]

In so far as this also applies to Being and Time, the analysis of Dasein and the tensions and paradoxes that arise within that analysis are themselves evidence of the essential character of Being. In part therefore, and this is developed in his later work, the meaning of Being in *Being and Time* is not approached directly but seen in the manner in which the analysis of Dasein proceeds. To use the language of the early Wittgenstein, the meaning of Being is shown and not said.

The hermeneutic and phenomenological method in *Being and Time* results in an analysis which develops not so much by making distinctions but by gradually developing a terminology which enables Heidegger to open up new perspectives. Heidegger's analysis is not trying to provide a ground for that which we can see is obvious, but to expand and bring to light that which we are not normally aware is even present. *Being and Time* as a result functions like an immensely intricate and complex story. The original framework develops as further details are added and refined. The book does not therefore conclude with a sense of resolution, as if everything were now fully decribed, but rather with a sense of emergence, having created a language in which a world is uncovered, but a world which cannot be defined and formalized.

The reflexive aspects of Heidegger's methodology have their outcome in the structure of *Being and Time*. One of the most fundamental distinctions that Heidegger makes is the one between the ontic and the ontological. The ontic world is the everyday world in which we all partake; it is the world which common sense regards as *the* world. It is the world of entities, of facts and information; the world that science investigates. The ontic world is not in any way strange to us; in fact to describe it is to describe the obvious. It is a world in which we find ourselves as individuals at a point in history, at a particular geographical position.

Set against this familiar world is the ontological world. The ontological world is the world of Being as opposed to the world of entities and beings. Since our concepts in general apply to the ontic world, a description of the ontological world is more difficult than describing 'the world of everydayness', and ultimately elusive. While Dasein as an entity, as an object, takes its place in the ontic world, it also takes part in the ontological world through its link with Being. In the ontological world Dasein does not find itself at a particular geographical position or at a particular point in time, for these are the product of the essential character of Dasein's Being. From an ontological point of view Dasein provides the space that Heidegger later refers to as a clearing, through which Being discloses itself.

Man is forced into being Dasein, hurled into the affliction of such Being, because the overpowering as such, in order to appear in its power, *requires* a place, a scene of disclosure. . . . Being itself hurls man into this breaking away, which drives him beyond himself to venture forth toward Being, to accomplish Being. . . .[36]

Heidegger is not concerned to analyse Dasein with regard to the ontic world. Such an analysis might be considered a section of psychology or anthropology. Heidegger's aim is to analyse the ontological character of Dasein as a means to uncover the nature of Being as a whole because, for Heidegger, Dasein is 'ontico-ontologically prior', by which he means that Dasein is unique among entities in the ontic world by being ontological.

The analysis of the Being of Dasein begins by examining one of the basic modes of Dasein – Being-in-the-world. Heidegger later examines other modes of Dasein such as Being-with-others, and Being-towards-death. From our everyday perspective Dasein finds itself within the world interacting with others and facing the possibility that at some indeterminate point in the future Dasein will no longer exist. This is not, however, the meaning that Heidegger refers to by Being-in-the-world, Being-with-others, and Being-towards-death. In each case Heidegger reinterprets these terms and transforms their significance. For example, in the mode of Dasein which Heidegger calls Being-in-the-world, Heidegger does not by 'world' mean the ontic world, nor by Being-in does he imply something akin to being inside (as if we might imagine that we were inside a room the size of the world). Nor is there any immediate way of saying what Heidegger does mean by Being-in-the-world, for all of the categories one might use to describe this mode of Dasein are ones that we employ in our description of the ontic world. To approach what is meant by Being-in-the-world we have gradually to move away from our traditional concepts, and this is how *Being and Time* proceeds.

Before we are in a position to understand the meaning of 'world', Heidegger introduces a new terminology to describe our relation to things. In the ontic world things, entities, are present-at-hand. Objects are discrete and passive and are simply present. Dasein, however, encounters things not as things but as equipment. Heidegger is not making the self-evident point that we are able to use objects-present-at-hand, but that the ontological world is made up of equipment and not of entities. Thus each item of equipment takes part in the totality of equipment which makes up the world. Heidegger goes on to develop the character of the relationship between Dasein and equipment. Dasein does not just bump into equipment in the way that we might be said to bump into things, but is said to have concernful dealings with equipment, and in so far as it has this relationship with equipment the equipment can be said to be ready-at-hand.

It is by further developing the character of the ready-to-hand and its relationship to the totality of equipment and to Dasein that Heidegger moves towards being able to describe what is meant by 'world'. It is through this gradual accretion of new terminology, which is explicated negatively against what we already understand, that the immense story of *Being and Time* can unfold. The question to which we will constantly return is whether this new conceptual framework has any content. Heidegger is not unaware of this potential criticism:

75

But have we not confined ourselves to negative assertions in all our attempts to determine the nature of this state of Being? Though this Being-in is supposedly so fundamental, we always keep hearing about what it is *not*. Yes indeed.[37]

There is a sense in which we can only ever hear about what Being is not, for if Being could be described it would no longer be Being. Sartre, in *Being and Nothingness*, followed this thought saying 'We have to deal with human reality as a being which is what it is not and which is not what it is.'[38] Thus what can on the one hand appear as the emptiness of Heidegger's categories, on the other is their effectiveness at capturing the elusiveness of Being.

By using this means of negative definition Heidegger is able to avoid, to a remarkably successful degree, the constraints of our present categories. He is not, however, able to escape from these categories entirely. Heidegger has to account for why the ontic world is commonly regarded as the 'real world'. The ontical categories must themselves be a necessary product of Being, and thus the initially straightforward distinction between the inauthenticity of the everyday world and the authenticity of the Being of Dasein begins to break down. The everyday world is thus also authentic, since it is also a product of Being.

This undifferentiated character of Dasein's everydayness is *not nothing*, but a positive phenomenal characteristic of this entity. . . . That which is ontically closest and well known, is ontologically farthest and not known at all; and its ontological signification is constantly overlooked.[39]

In *Being and Time* Heidegger retains the distinction between the inauthentic and the authentic, the ontic and the ontological, but they become successively more intertwined. Thus the present-at-hand and the ready-to-hand which at first are presented as wholly different are seen to be dependent on each other and, furthermore, the priority of the ready-to-hand is denied:

To lay bare what is just present-at-hand and no more, cognition must first penetrate *beyond* what is ready-to-hand in our concern. *Readiness-to-hand is the way in which entities as they are 'in themselves' are defined ontologico-categorially*. Yet only by reason of something present at-hand 'is there' anything ready-to-hand.[40]

The seeming obscurity that results from the collapsing of his own distinctions is the result of his view that immediate access to the truth is not possible. So long as we regard the authentic world as the 'true' world, the distinctions between the ontological and the ontic can be easily maintained. From this point of view the ontic is no more than a mistake or naive simplification. But Heidegger is not wishing to argue that the authentic world is the true world. Instead the tension between authenticity and inauthenticity itself becoms necessary. While Heidegger may have moved beyond our traditional categories he has neither reached, nor wishes to claim to have reached, *the* categories. Since he is in search of something wholly other, that other must constantly recede. Just when we think we have understood what Heidegger might mean by Being we are reminded that the meaning of Being is at one further remove. Yet distinctions that Heidegger does make are made on the basis of some prior understanding of what we mean by Being. The reflexive paradox in this position is thus a double one – we are incapable of being able to describe Being and we must already know what it is or we could not move towards it. Even in *Being and Time* Heidegger is explicitly aware of this tension:

Whenever a phenomenological concept is drawn from primordial sources, there is a possibility that it may degenerate if communicated in the form of an assertion. It gets understood in an empty way and is passed on losing its indigenous character, and becoming a free-floating thesis. Even in the concrete work of phenomenology itself there lurks the possibility that what has been primordially 'within our grasp' may become hardened so that we can no longer grasp it. And the difficulty of this kind of research lies in making it self-critical in a positive sense.[41]

The reflexive character of Heidegger's method thus shows itself in the structure of *Being and Time* by the distinctions being constantly revised: what at first appears separate and opposite becomes linked and interdependent; the move towards Being never comes any closer. We are continually being given an impression of what Being consists of, yet as we near the point of being able to grasp it so it once again recedes. This is, however, not a shortcoming of *Being and Time* but a necessary result of the overall method and the reflexive character of the object of the research: 'Being contracts into the beings it makes manifest and hides by the very fact that it reveals.'[42]

Like Nietzsche, Heidegger does not set out to solve the problems of reflexivity but to use them as a positive means of showing the limitations of our previous outlook and of moving beyond that outlook. Although *Being and Time* appears much more systematic than

Nietzsche's works, this should not lead us to think that Heidegger regarded it as metaphysical, in the sense of providing a final decription of the character of the world and of our being. Heidegger's escape from metaphysics is attempted by the use of his hermeneutic method and the unstable and reflexive character of the system and the key terms that he explicates. These two aspects are inevitably linked in so far as the structure of *Being and Time* is a product of its method. In *Being and Time*, therefore, Heidegger uses an essentially self-critical method and a self-undermining structure while presenting a coherent system. Instead of regarding reflexivity as a negative and destructive force, Heidegger sees in the reflexive circle the means of achieving that which is otherwise unachievable: ' . . . it is not to be reduced to the level of a vicious circle, or even of a circle which is merely tolerated. In the circle is hidden a positive possibility of the most primordial kind of knowing.'[43] Thus in apparent contrast to Nietzsche the reflexivity of *Being and Time*, far from resulting in theoretical anarchy, is incorporated into a highly structured system.

Language and the later Heidegger

In his later writings Heidegger gradually moves away from the concepts and systematic character of *Being and Time*. It is almost as if the reflexivity, which in *Being and Time* is kept within bounds and halted before it undermines the conceptual distinctions entirely, is slowly unleashed. While in *Being and Time* we move towards uncovering the meaning of Being and do not arrive, nevertheless Being itself appears to retain a coherent character. By the time of the *Introduction to Metaphysics* (1935) Being has taken on a more paradoxical character:

Thus the word 'Being' is indefinite in meaning and yet we understand it definitely. 'Being' proves to be totally indeterminate and at the same time highly determinate. From the standpoint of the usual logic we have here an obvious contradiction. Something that contradicts itself cannot be.[44]

After the war Heidegger uses the technique of writing the word 'Being' with a cross through it, to indicate that we are not to take the word as referring to an object that has a unitary character. Later Heidegger almost abandons the use of the term, replacing it with preferable alternatives: ' . . . thinking must first overcome the habit of yielding to the view that we are thinking here of "Being" as appropriation. But appropriation is different in nature, because it is richer than any conceivable definition of Being.'[45]

The growing indeterminacy and ineffability of Being is indicative of the abandonment of the system of *Being and Time* as a whole. In this respect parallels can be drawn between Heidegger and Wittgenstein. In both cases their early work presents a complete system and from then on they move away from this formal framework. The fundamental difference is that while Wittgenstein concludes that it is not possible to make general philosophical claims at all, Heidegger insists that while these are never satisfactory they are nevertheless the high point of human endeavour. He also argues that at a certain level these are unavoidable. Certainly as far as Wittgenstein is concerned it can be argued that the attempt to avoid general philosophical claims is itself based on an implicit general claim that general philosophical claims are not possible. Nevertheless Heidegger's assertion of the importance of the philosophical enterprise carries with it the risk of our being left with empty rhetoric.

The gradual abandonment of the system of *Being and Time* is mirrored by Heidegger's increasing stress on the role and importance of language. The reflexivity of the later writings is, therefore, predominantly a reflexivity of language and the text, rather than a reflexivity of Dasein or Being. This shift of focus is subsequently continued by Derrida, and it is the transition from a reflexivity of the subject to a reflexivity of language which makes the question of reflexivity so insistent and so all-embracing.

The seeds of Heidegger's later views on language are to be found in *Being and Time*. Signs, the constituent parts of language, are here described as items of equipment. In this respect they are simply part of the totality of equipment that makes up the world. The sign however is unique as an item of equipment, for it is the item of equipment through which the totality of equipment is made visible.

A sign is not a Thing which stands to another Thing in the relationship of indicating; it is rather *an item of equipment which explicitly raises a totality of equipment into our circumspection so that together with it the worldly character of the ready-to-hand announces itself.*[46]

Thus even in *Being and Time* the sign is that through which the world is made apparent, but more importantly the status of the sign itself is obscure because of its reflexive character. The sign makes apparent the totality of equipment but, as part of that totality, it also makes itself apparent. In announcing the world the sign reflexively announces itself. In so doing, instead of merely indicating Being, it is integrally linked with Being.

In *An Introduction to Metaphysics* Heidegger agues that it is only through language that there is Being at all: 'For words and language are not wrappings in which things are packed for the commerce of those who write and speak. It is in words and language that things first come into Being and are.'[47] Heidegger later reformulates this in the phrase 'language is the house of Being'. The subsequent centrality that Heidegger gives to the topic of language is due not only to language being seen to provide the space for Being, but also to the reflexive abyss that follows in its wake. For to make the claim that 'it is in words and language that things first come into Being and are' is to use language. Only through language are we able to talk of 'Being' at all. 'Being' is 'only' a word. If it is through language that we have Being, then it is language which gives Being to the word 'Being'. At this point it is no longer clear what we might mean by either 'language' or 'Being'. It is as if through language there miraculously is something, and yet it is unclear what that something is – since we remain caught within language in our attempt to describe that something.

Heidegger only confronts this problem directly in his writings after 1945. Previously in *An Introduction to Metaphysics* Heidegger made the initial move of regarding the origin of language as a mystery and its fundamental nature as poetic rather than representational.

The origin of language is in essence mysterious. And this means that language can only have arisen from the overpowering, the strange and terrible, through man's departure into Being. In this departure language was Being, embodied in the word: poetry. Language is the primordial poetry in which a people speaks Being.[48]

However, from this point on Heidegger adopts a number of different strategies by which to investigate the phenomenon of language.

In the same way that the nature of Being was unclear so now it is the nature of language that is unclear. By 'language' Heidegger does not mean what we would normally understand by this term. He is not referring to the object of linguistic science but to that which announces that there is a world. Words provide a space for Being, and 'language' is the term which tries to describe the very provision of that space. As such it tries to describe its own space – the space which allows the word 'language' to describe itself. Thus 'language', as Heidegger uses the term, carries within it a wellspring of Being. For in the enunciation of the word 'language' there is the creation of something which itself refers to the nature of that creation. 'The sentence "language is language" leaves us to hover over an abyss as long as we endure what it says.'[49] Language thus reflexively tries to say itself, for in uttering the word 'language' we attempt to say what it is that enables us to say anything at all, and through which there is anything at all. As with Being, therefore, the investigation of language is in search of the object that it is investigating.

When we reflect on language *qua* language, we have abandoned the traditional procedure of language study. . . . Instead of explaining language in terms of one thing or another, and thus running away from it, the way to language intends to let language be experienced as language.[50]

Faced with this reflexive circle Heidegger seeks to move towards the nature of language by abandoning the assertoric, representational mode of ordinary discourse. He asks us to 'step back from the thinking that merely represents – that is explains – to the thinking that responds and recalls'.[51] Thus all of the various strategies that Heidegger uses to try to come close to the nature of language are attempts to speak in a non-representational way. The avoidance of representation, however, involves its own reflexive circularity. For example, one strategy that Heidegger employs is to use the rhetoric of hints and gestures rather than claims and assertions. He hints at the nature of language rather than asserting the nature of language. There is always the risk, however, that the nature of a hint will itself become definite, and in being definite as a hint will lose the character of a true hint, in which the nature of hinting is non-representational and essentially mysterious. Hence the interchange in the essay 'A dialogue on language' between a Japanese, referred to as J, and Heidegger, referred to as I (the Inquirer):

J: When you now speak of hints, this freeing word emboldens me to name to you the word by which to us the nature of language is – how shall I say . . .
I: . . . perhaps hinted.
J: That is to the point. But even so I fear that to call your 'house of Being' a hint

81

might tempt you and me to elaborate the notion of hinting into a guiding concept in which we can then bundle up everying.[52]

The use of a dialogue form in this essay is another mechanism by which Heidegger hopes to be able to keep representation at bay. The meaning of a dialogue allows for ambiguity and can more easily avoid the risk of being taken as an assertoric statement than a formal essay. In this essay the parties to the dialogue discuss the way in which western thought turns everything into an object, but because of the dialogue form Heidegger is able to avoid the reflexive implication that this essay has itself objectified the character of western thought. Similarly the parties discuss the way in which one must avoid giving any direct answer to the nature of language. The dialogue by its hesitation, and the essay through its form, try to avoid the appearance of doing precisely that – namely – giving an answer. Heidegger thus wishes to replace representational language with an alternative, but that alternative is necessarily unnameable, and there is always the suspicion that however much Heidegger hints, and hesitates, and adopts non-assertoric forms, if he is to have any content to this alternative he must present something; and in presenting that something he has once again been reduced to representational language.

We may be tempted to regard Heidegger as investigating a reflexive circle – the attempt to move towards the nature of language, already incorporates its own failure. Such an interpretation is, however, to provide an account of a task which for Heidegger must remain shrouded. Heidegger argues that even to see this circle as a mystery is to give it a specific form and character and thus deprive it of its fundamental mystery:

J: We Japanese have – I think I may say so – an innate understanding for your kind of reserve. A mystery is a mystery only when it does not even come out *that* mystery is at work.
I: To those who are superficial and in a hurry, no less than to those who are deliberate and reflective, it must look as though there were no mystery anywhere.
J: But we are surrounded by the danger, not just of talking too loudly about the mystery, but of missing its working.
I: To guard against the purity of the mystery's wellspring seems to me the hardest of all.[53]

Thus it is to the circle and poetic descriptions of this circle that

Heidegger turns in order to uncover the nature of language. To call this circle a circle is inevitably to attempt to escape from the circle and to fail in this attempt in the same way that to call the origin of language a mystery is to remove the mystery. Nevertheless if we are to call this centre anything at all it is to this reflexive movement that we return.

J: It seems to me that now we are moving in a circle. A dialogue from language must be called for from out of language's reality. How can it do so, without first entering into a hearing that at once reaches that reality?

I: I once called this strange relation the hermeneutic circle . . .

J: Did you not say earlier that this circle is inevitable, and that, instead of trying to avoid it as an alleged logical contradiction, we must follow it?

I: Yes.[54]

In a later essay 'The way to language' the circularity of language provides the focus and is the means by which Heidegger attempts to move towards language. At the beginning of the essay and close to the end Heidegger refers to the following quotation from Novalis: 'The peculiar property of language, namely that language is concerned exclusively with itself – precisely that is known to no one.' In this claim we not only have the circularity of language but a claim which is immediately paradoxical by apparently stating something that is known to no one, including presumably the one who is making the statement. Reflexivity is no longer a negative force but the means through which the essential nature of language can be sought. It is in the whirlpool that is generated by such claims, in their entire collapsing of representation that Heidegger catches a glimpse of the primary source and power of language.

Language is – language, speech. Language speaks. If we let ourselves fall into the abyss denoted by this sentence, we do not go tumbling into emptiness. We fall upward to a height. Its loftiness opens up a depth. The two span a realm in which we would like to become at home, so as to find a residence, a dwelling place for the life of man.[55]

In order to open up the depth that lies hidden behind the husks of meaning that we normally use, Heidegger tries to take us to the place of the mystery of our words. He tries to do this through poetry, through a repetition of the paradox of 'language', and by an attempted description of the mystery which itself dissolves since it must also remain mysterious. With Wittgenstein he sees us as trapped within language, but unlike Wittgenstein he also regards our attempt to describe that predicament, or hint at the character of our state, as a task which is closest to our own human being.

In order to be who we are, we human beings remain committed to and within the being of language, and can never step out of it and look at it from somewhere else. Thus we always see the nature of language only to the extent to which language itself has us in view, has appropriated us to itself. That we cannot know the nature of language – know it according to the traditional concept of knowledge defined in terms of cognition as representation – is not a defect, however, but rather an advantage by which we are favoured with a special realm, that realm where we, who are needed and used to speak language, dwell as *mortals*.[56]

It is through poetry and by standing over the abyss of reflexivity that we have the possibility of access to this realm that once Heidegger would have called Being. In his essay 'Language' Heidegger repeats what would usually be regarded as the most empty of tautologies – 'language is language'; in 'The Way to Language' he uses the formula 'we try to speak about speech *qua* speech'. In both cases he calls on the different levels of meaning within the same term to destabilize the meaning of the whole. That destabilization is, however, in a certain sense *the* meaning of the phrase. For held in that destabilization is the web of language, and thus the web of Being. The reflexive circle is thus a product of the essential form of language. 'The circle is a special case of our web of language. It is meaningful, because the direction and manner of the circling motion are determined by language itself, by a movement within language.'[57]

Poetry has a pre-eminent position for Heidegger because poetry makes no pretence at representation and is thus able to move towards the web of language that we find ourselves part of, and which we speak. In the 1940s and early 1950s Heidegger used poetic forms to describe a world of universal Being like that of *Being and Time*.

Whatever becomes a thing occurs out of the ringing of the world's mirror-play. Only when – all of a sudden, presumably – world worlds as a world, only then does the ring shine forth, the joining from which the ringing of earth and heaven, divinities and mortals, wrests itself free for that compliancy of simple oneness.[58]

84

However, as Heidegger's concern with language becomes more central, poetry ceases to be a special and privileged form of language, but instead language becomes essentially poetic. Heidegger is thus trying to lead us to use language in a new way, a way which we might call poetic, but which by describing it thus we have already destroyed.

Heidegger wishes to change our relation to language but he cannot tell us in what way it should change. Perhaps we could say that he shows us how this change is made by operating from the other side of the change. Heidegger started out by forming new words to escape the constraints of the tradition. The new meanings came from an excavation of the old. Later he turned to poetic forms and paradoxes. In the end he is left with trying to shift our relation to language but without giving us any idea of how this is to take place other than to indicate by his manner and mode of speech what is involved. It is almost as if we can only 'catch on' and there is no way in which we can be shown how this is to be done. 'We might perhaps prepare a little for the change in our relation to language. Perhaps this experience might awaken: All reflective thinking is poetic, and all poetry in turn is a kind of thinking.'[59] Once we have moved into the new relation to language all is the same and yet all is different. The same terms are used, the same phrases expressed, but instead of implying a world of discreteness, of particulars and absolutes, there is a world whose character is to evade capture. Heidegger ends his essay 'The Way to Language' with a quotation from von Humboldt: 'Then the old shell is filled with new meaning, the old coinage conveys something different, the old laws of syntax are used to hint at a differently graduated sequence of ideas.' The quotation has the further reflexive edge that it is itself 'an old shell filled with new meaning' – a phrase previously used elsewhere that Heidegger employs 'to hint at a differently graduated sequence of ideas'.

Heidegger's use of reflexivity thus shifts from its incorporation into his method and the stucture of his theory to providing the indication of the essential character of language. The entire Heideggerian project may, however, seem absurd. For the reflexive paradox and the resultant ineffability with which Heidegger ends is there in the beginning. From one perspective Heidegger sets up his project in such a way that he could never succeed; it is hardly surprising, therefore, that there is nothing more concrete in the end than at the beginning. Is there anything more here than a form of religious faith which on the one hand tells us the truth in one bound and yet which is never able to tell us any more? If it is possible to have access to truths in some straightforward way, the Heideggerian project must fall to this interpretation. For the Heideggerian project only has weight if in some way there is no alternative. To attempt to achieve that which is defined as being unachievable is a ludicrous enterprise if it is possible to do otherwise. It is Heidegger's claim that it is not possible to do otherwise. To be human is to have fallen into this condition, and it is in the tension between the attempt to escape our limitations and the inevitable impossibility of such an escape that we express that which is closest to ourselves. Heidegger does not therefore try to provide us with an answer to reflexivity, for it is the key to, and the character of, our Being, our language.

Notes

1   M. Heidegger, *What Is Called Thinking*, translated by J. Glenn Gray (Harper and Row 1968), p. 62.
2   ibid., p. 72.
3   F. Nietzsche, *Thus Spake Zarathustra* (T. N. Foulis 1909), sec. 42 (Redemption).
4   F. Nietzsche, *The Will To Power*, translated by Walter Kauffmann and J. R. Hollingdale (Vintage Books 1968), sec. 617; and also *Thus Spake Zarathustra*, sec. 42.
5   'Who is Nietzsche's Zarathustra', *Review of Metaphysics*, no. 20 (1967), translated by Bernard Magnus.
6   M. Heidegger, 'A Dialogue On Language', from *On the Way to Language*, translated by Peter D. Hertz (Harper and Row 1971), p. 51.
7   Heidegger, *What is Called Thinking*, p. 80.
8   M. Heidegger, *An Introduction to Metaphysics*, translated by Ralph Manheim (Yale University Press 1959), p. 78.
9   M. Heidegger, *Letter On Humanism*, tr. Edgar Lohner, in *Philosophy in the Twentieth Century*, vol. 3, edited by William Barrett and Henry Aiken (Random House 1962), p. 282.
10 Heidegger, *An Introduction to Metaphysics*, p. 162.
11 H. Gadamer, *Truth and Method* (Sheed and Ward).
12 H. Gadamer, 'Historicity of Understanding', from *Heidegger*

and Modern Philosophy, critical essays edited by Michael Murray (Yale University Press 1978), p. 165.

13 R. Rorty, 'Overcoming the Tradition: Heidegger and Dewey', from *Consequences of Pragmatism* (Harvester Press 1982), p. 52.

14 Heidegger, *An Introduction to Metaphysics*, p. 162.

15 Heidegger, *What Is Called Thinking*, p. 52.

16 Heidegger, *An Introduction to Metaphysics*, p. 51.

17 M. Heidegger, *Poetry, Language, Thought*, translations and introduction by Albert Hofstader (Harper and Row 1971), p. 208.

18 Heidegger, *An Introduction to Metaphysics*, p. 42.

19 ibid., p. 7.

20 ibid., p. 29.

21 ibid., p. 5.

22 ibid., p. 6.

23 ibid., p. 8.

24 Richardson, *Heidegger through Phenomenology to Thought*, in Heidegger's letter to Richardson.

25 M. Heidegger, *On the Way to Language*, p. 7.

26 M. Heidegger, *Being and Time*, translated by John Macquarrie and Edward Robinson (Basil Blackwell 1973), p. 50.

27 ibid., p. 59.

28 ibid., p. 58.

29 ibid., p. 51.

30 ibid., p. 59.

31 ibid., p. 59.

32 ibid., p. 87.

33 ibid., p. 32.

34 ibid., p. 106.

35 ibid., p. 40.

36 Heidegger, *An Introduction to Metaphysics*, pp. 162–3.

37 Heidegger, *Being and Time*, p. 85.

38 J.-P. Satre, *Being and Nothingness*, translated by H. E. Barnes (Methuen 1957), p. 58.

39 Heidegger, *Being and Time*, p. 69.

40 ibid., p. 101.

41 ibid., p. 60.

42 Richardson, *Heidegger through Phenomenology to Thought*.

43 Heidegger, *Being and Time*, p. 195.

44   Heidegger, *An Introduction to Metaphysics*, p. 78.
45   Heidegger, *On the Way to Language*, p. 129.
46   Heidegger, *Being and Time*, p. 110.
47   Heidegger, *An Introduction to Metaphysics*, p. 13.
48   ibid., p. 171.
49   Heidegger, *Poetry, Language, Thought*, p. 191.
50   Heidegger, *On the Way to Language*, p. 119.
51   Heidegger, *Poetry, Language, Thought*, p. 181.
52   Heidegger, *On the Way to Language*, p. 24.
53   ibid., p. 50.
54   ibid., p. 51.
55   Heidegger, *Poetry, Language, Thought*, p. 182.
56   Heidegger, *On the Way to Language*, p. 134.
57   ibid., p. 113.
58   Heidegger, *Poetry, Language, Thought*, p. 182.
59   Heidegger, *On Way to Language*, p. 136.

Further reading

Heidegger's central work *Being and Time*, tr. John Macquarrie and Edward Robinson (London 1962; Oxford 1967), is particularly difficult. A more obvious starting-point is therefore his *Introduction to Metaphysics*, tr. Ralph Manheim (Yale University Press 1959). The first section of this book 'The fundamental question' provides perhaps the best overall description of the Heideggerian project.

Of his later writings the collections *Poetry, Language, Thought*, tr. Albert Hofstadter (New York: Harper and Row 1971), and *On the Way to Language*, tr. Peter Hertz and Joan Stambaugh (New York: Harper and Row 1971), give a good indication of Heidegger's altered perspective. In general, as an introduction to Heidegger's writings, his works on other philosophers, particularly on Nietzsche, should be avoided. However, to obtain any greater understanding of Heidegger, *Being and Time* is essential. (A note of warning: Heidegger's writings were published in a very different order to their inception – do not be misled by the date of publication.)

As far as secondary material is concerned Richard Rorty's article: 'Overcoming the Tradition: Heidegger and Dewey' in the collection *Richard Rorty: Consequences of Pragmatism* (Harvester Press 1982) gives a good impression of Heidegger's position in a remarkably short space.

The three essays on Heidegger in Gadamer's *Philosophical Hermeneutics*, tr. D. E. Lange (Calif.: California University Press 1976), are to be highly recommended – especially 'Heidegger's later philosophy', which Heidegger himself described as giving 'a decisive hint'. Introductory accounts of Heidegger's work include J. L. Mehta's *The Philosophy of Martin Heidegger*, (New York: Harper and Row 1971), and George Steiner's *Heidegger* (Fontana Modern Masters 1978) which includes a useful short bibliography. A book worthy of note for those who want more than an introduction: William Richardson's *Heidegger: through Phenomenology to Thought* (The Hague 1963), (Heidegger's preface to this book is of particular interest, and provides an overview of Heidegger's writing as a whole), while the best collection of essays is to be found in Michael Murray's *Heidegger and Modern Philosophy: Critical Essays* (Yale University Press 1978). Within this collection the essays by Carnap, 'The Overcoming of Metaphysics', and Ryle, 'Heidegger's Sein und Zeit', give an indication of the type of criticisms of Heidegger that are prominent in the analytic tradition. An influential critique of Heidegger within continental philosophy can be found in T. W. Adorno's, *Jargon of Authenticity*.

4

Derrida

Once upon a time a story was told. It went as follows:

The epoch in which we live, the epoch which is now drawing to a close, is characterized by a belief in the Book. In this Book is held a description of our world. It is a true and accurate description of how things are, and of how they were. This Book is in the process of being completed; at present we have only fragments. Fragments to which others are being added – painstakingly determined through research and analysis.

The belief in the existence of the Book has been responsible for the way in which we have interpreted the world, and underlies all of our thinking. The Book and the fragments are however mythical. The belief in the Book, although necessary, has had no foundation. We must now abandon this belief, but in doing so we must be careful not to initiate a belief in a new Book which will be seen to be more accurate than the previous one.

This story does not constitute a fragment or even a segment of a fragment in such a Book, for the Book is not even possible. Nor is there an essence, or final meaning, of this, or any other story which could be told by others – for there is never a single unified story, but a plenitude of stories that play and jostle with the other stories of our time. Beware those who would claim otherwise.

If having been told this story one was to relate it to someone else, a problem would arise – assuming the story could not be remembered word for word. Our difficulties would stem from the claim made within the story that the story itself has no single identifiable meaning. In our attempt to relate the story we would inevitably attempt to convey what appeared to us to be its salient points. One of those salient points, however, would consist in the denial that the narrative had any salient points. If we were to recount the story on these lines – that the central point of this story was that it had no central point, we would have reintroduced the very aspect that the story denied. It would after all have a central point, a final meaning, namely that there was no final meaning. The story, in denying an essence, cannot without risking absurdity be regarded as asserting that denial as its essence. How then is it possible to relate such a story? One would like to say how is it possible to convey its meaning, or its central significance, but to do so would be to undermine one of the themes of the story – but perhaps even to call it a theme is to say too much.

One might be tempted to think that the story could be described in a general way, that it could be said to be 'mystical' or 'allegorical'. To say this would, however, be to imply that there was a language in which the character of the story could be described definitively. Judged by the criteria provided in the story, such a description would be an attempt to provide a fragment that could be placed in the Book. It would be an attempt to provide a 'true description of how things are'; to give an account of the character of the story which could remain. Within the context of the story the possibility of providing such fragments of knowledge is described as illusory. This only generates a problem for those who believe in the story – for those who don't, and who regard fragments of knowledge as possible, there is no difficulty in providing a general description of the story in the sort of terms suggested. So long as we can resort to a meta-discourse in order to describe the story we can avoid the paradoxes that would otherwise be present. Within the discourse of the story, however, the problems associated with describing its content remain.

One further point about this story should be noted: for the very reasons that make the story difficult to relate, if one was an adherent of such a story it would be unclear to what one was adhering. It could not simply be that our society has necessarily believed in the existence of the Book although in fact this Book does not exist – for such a view would be typical of the fragments that make up the Book and which are precisely denied in the story. Nor could an adherent of this story assert the non-existence of knowledge. Such an assertion would be immediately paradoxical – to have knowledge that there could be no knowledge. The adherent is thus apparently left in the uncomfortable position of adhering to something which he or she is unable to describe – other than perhaps to recite the story word for word.

For the moment let us leave the relationship between this story and Derrida's own philosophical position vague; whatever else, for reasons allied to those laid out above, there would be something decidedly unsatisfactory in saying that this story was a simplified version of Derrida's 'position'. Some of the problems in relating the story, however, are similar to the difficulties encountered in describing Derrida's work. They may therefore give some idea of why many who have tried to give an account of Derrida have begun with a consideration of how to begin, or of how the account itself should be read. This seemingly tedious self-consciousness is the product of the character of Derrida's text and the explicitly reflexive self-awareness that permeates all aspects of his writing.

All our comments about Derrida will therefore be provisional, in the sense that they may be rejected at a later point in the light of further examination of his work, in much the same way that one might begin to describe the story of the Book, only to later cancel the first description in favour of an alternative which might in turn be cancelled in favour of another.

Reflexivity – as critique

Derrida's first major writings were an examination of Husserl, the founder of phenomenology, and provided a critique of his position. In so far as Heidegger can be regarded as engaging in a similar enterprise, the two have much in common. Derrida, however, is concerned from the outset with the role and function of language, and writes in the aftermath of the structuralist analyses of Saussure and the development of semiology. Thus, if in Heidegger we see reflexivity shift its focus from the Being of Dasein to language, in Derrida the full force of reflexivity is revealed because language and the text have become the only arena.

Like Nietzsche's, Derrida's writing can be seen as having a negative and a positive aspect. If the central role of reflexivity is not recognized the text appears not only opaque but almost intentionally obtuse and contradictory. One can distinguish three distinct, but connected, roles that reflexivity plays in Derrida's text: as the negative, deconstructive aspect of Derrida's work; as the motor that determines the shape of the positive theory; and as the destroyer of that theory as it finally turns back on itself.

If we begin with the role that reflexivity plays in the negative, deconstructive side of Derrida's writing, we should not be misled into thinking that this provides a simple precursor, or foundation for, the positive theory; it is both the grounds for, and the result of, that positive theory. It is for this reason that his books are a combination of his own philosophy and the criticism of the works of others (if for a moment we can allow such a distinction – one which Derrida himself would challenge). Possibly for this reason, his work has been more widely read in Britain and North America in the field of literary criticism than in philosophy.

Deconstruction, at its simplest, consists of reading a text so closely that the conceptual distinctions, on which the text relies, are shown to fail on account of the inconsistent and paradoxical employment of these very concepts within the text as a whole. Thus the text is seen to fall by its own criteria – the standards or definitions which the text sets up are used reflexively to unsettle and shatter the original distinctions. Derrida has used this technique against Husserl, Rousseau, Saussure, Plato, Freud and others. Inherent in his method, however, is the view that it could be applied to any text – with the possible exception of Nietzsche, whom Derrida interprets as having already employed this technique against himself.

Deconstruction is not simply the demonstration of inconsistencies in a text – if it was it would hardly be a radical new method of criticism. Its power comes from the claim that any text can be deconstructed, so long as, in Derrida's phrase, it remains within 'the metaphysics of presence'. The connection between the method of deconstruction and the 'theory' of the metaphysics of presence is, as we shall see, a vital one. Without it the force of a deconstructive reading, by a reflexive application of the text to itself, is lost. It is in Derrida's works on Husserl, the first two books that he published, that this link is most clearly argued.

In much the same way that Descartes had sought a ground of certainty from which it was possible to authenticate scientific knowledge, Husserl attempted to provide a pure logic which could serve to validate a new well-founded science. In this respect Husserl's project also has similarities with Wittgenstein's aims in the *Tractatus*. Both philosophers were attempting to provide the essential character of the world (which for Husserl was the pure form of experience), and in each case an analysis of language was a vital element in the project. For Wittgenstein this involved describing the structure of language necessary for language to be able to operate at all. This essential structure consisted of names in propositions in logical space, which pictured facts made up of objects in the world. Once this was outlined it was then possible for Wittgenstein to lay down the conditions for a meaningful sentence, and thus to limit what it was possible to say about the world. By this means we could clear our theories of the meaningless, being confident that the remainder, although possibly false, had determinate sense. Similarly, Husserl wished to remove the context-dependent element in language and describe the essential, pure, logical grammar that would provide the bedrock on which a sound edifice could be built. The method for doing this was the technique Husserl termed 'the transcendental reduction' by which the empirical was gradually stripped away to leave the essential form of consciousness.

Since Husserl's project was to provide certainty through a pure logical grammar, and thus avert what he regarded as a crisis in modern science, his theory of language and its relationship to the world was central. Characteristically, Derrida takes issue with, and examines most closely, a distinction that Husserl makes in the first paragraph of his first major work. The work was called *The Logical Investigations*, from which, as Derrida points out, the whole of phenomenology flowed. But it is Derrida's contention that this first distinction is necessarily flawed, and that the moves that Husserl needs to make in order to maintain the opposition are responsible for the form of the entire theoretical edifice that he finally erects.

This distinction, that Derrida examines with such persistence in *Speech and Phenomena*, is the one between 'Ausdruck' and 'Anzeichen', between 'expression' and 'indication'. Husserl regards these as two senses of the single word 'sign'. This opposition is related to the Fregean distinction between 'sense' and 'reference' which has been influential almost to the point of providing the framework within which, in the Anglo-Saxon world, the philosophy of language has developed. But Husserl's distinction is significantly different – in fact he explicitly makes no distinction between 'Sinn' and 'Bedeutung' in the Fregean sense. Husserl's distinction is related to the function of the sign. The expression, linked to the intention of the speaker, is what we might call the pure meaning of the sign, and as such is distinguished from indication, a pointing or indicating function which could occur without any intentional meaning. It is in the form of pure expression, in the pure intent or meaning of the speaker abstracted from any empirical content, that Husserl sees the pure logical grammar.

Derrida's claim is that this distinction, without which the whole Husserlian project could not begin, cannot be upheld. Pure expression will always involve an indicative element, and however much Husserl tries to keep out the indicative it will of necessity creep back. This reappearance of the indicative, Derrida will argue, is demonstrated by Husserl's own text; thus the distinction which Husserl initially erects is shown by the ensuing text to have always failed. Right from the start, Derrida points out, the terms are distinct and yet entangled:

Husserl speaks first of an addition or juxtaposition of function: 'signs in the sense of indications *do not express anything*, unless they happen to fulfill a meaning *as well as* an indicative function'. But several lines further he speaks of an intimate involvement, an entanglement. This word will often reappear at decisive moments and this is not fortuitous.[1]

Husserl, in trying to isolate pure expression from any indicative element, considers the activity of a solitary mind. For here, devoid of any empirical context, Husserl can attempt to remove all traces of indication leaving only the pure logical form of the expression. Thus expression, which is founded in intentional communication, para-doxically, finds its purest form when it is cut off from any external factors at all. While in this pure logical grammar Husserl finds the structure of experience as a whole, Derrida argues for the impossi-bility of such a pure origin. Expression is hopelessly entwined with indication and therefore the goal of the pure origin and form is unattainable. Derrida's argument to this effect is reminiscent of Wittgenstein's private language argument:'A sign is never an event, if by event we mean an irreplaceable and irreversible empirical particular.'[2] Derrida's point is that a sign is necessarily repetitive; if it were not possible to repeat it it could no longer be a sign. Thus, in order to be a sign Husserl's pure expression in the solitary mind must be capable of repetition – but for this to be the case the conditions which Husserl sets up for the production of the pure expression are broken – the sign cannot remain as a pure product of the imagination, but must be linked in to the network of indicative signs. In Husserl's terminology the sign is forced to have a fictive element in its effective usage.

The deconstruction of Husserl's distinction between expression and indication is only one example of many other similar exercises in

95

which Derrida uses the internal logic of a text to demonstrate the inadequacy of a vital distinction on which it relies. In his critique of Rousseau, Derrida attempts to show that a whole range of distinctions, between the primitive and civilized, natural and non-natural, North and South, articulation and accentuation, melody and harmony, fail to retain their character as opposites, which are necessary in order to achieve their purpose. Thus Rousseau's assertion of the primacy of melody over harmony is shown to falter from the very beginning as melody, in order to be a melody, must already implicitly involve harmony. Above all, in his analyses of Lévi-Strauss and Saussure as well as Rousseau, it is the distinction between speech and writing which is deconstructed. Although, at times, Derrida simply appears to be asserting the reverse of that which is claimed in the text – harmony and not melody is primary, writing and not speech is prior – his aim is not to invert the claims of the text but to demonstrate that the opposition on which they are based is an impossible one. Thus his demonstration that speech has been prioritized over writing from the Greeks through to the present day, is not aimed at showing that writing was prior and takes a primary role (although in the process of the argument, Derrida does occasionally take up this position), but that the opposition between speech and writing cannot stand. Speech is shown to be inevitably bound up with writing; speech is always already writing. Later we will look more closely at the extended use of the term 'writing' employed by Derrida to draw this apparently baffling conclusion. For the moment we should note that in this respect deconstruction appears to be wholly negative since it does not challenge the text by asserting an alternative – by arguing for a different conclusion – but by taking apart the structure of the text and demonstrating its failings and paradoxes.

This first aspect of Derrida's use of reflexivity, that of turning a text back on itself, would nevertheless be little more than a dextrous play on words were it not for the associated 'theory' of the metaphysics of presence. This 'theory' (the reason for the quotation marks will become apparent later), finds in the deconstruction of a text both its outcome and its 'proof'. It is Derrida's contention that Husserl, along with almost all other philosophers, relies on the assumption of an immediately available arena of certainty. This origin and foundation of their theories is presence. In Husserl's case the search for the form of pure expression is at the same time a search for that which is immediately present; thus implicitly, by being present in an unmediated way and present to itself, it is undeniably certain. Derrida denies the possibility of this presence, and in so doing removes the ground from which he argues philosophers have in general proceeded.

By denying presence Derrida is denying that there is a present, in the sense of a single definable moment which is 'now'. He is, however, doing more than making a metaphysical point about time. From Zeno to F. H. Bradley, many philosophers have argued that regarding time as a series of separate instants leads to paradoxes. In *Being and Time* Heidegger had abandoned the common-sense view of time as a linear series of moments, or presents, in favour of viewing time as a structural characteristic of our being. Derrida, however, is trying not to provide an alternative description of time, but to undermine what he regards as the metaphysical attachment to presence.

For Derrida the present is the province of the known. We may be unsure of what took place in the past, of what may take place in the future, or of what is taking place elsewhere, but we rely on our knowledge of the present– the here and now. (It is worth noting that 'present' has both the sense of present in time, and present in space.) Philosophers from Descartes onwards have been aware of sceptical arguments against our knowledge of the present, but only in the sense of knowledge of the present external world. Thus although we might not be certain of the character of the present external world, we can be certain of the present perceptual world as it is happening to us. Relying on the certainty of our knowledge of this immediate present some philosophers have been concerned to demonstrate how we can be sure of our knowledge of the external world – knowledge of the internal world being assumed. Such sceptical questions concerned philosophers as diverse as Russell and Husserl. By challenging access to the present, Derrida is posing a threat to both positivism and phenomenology.

To understand what Derrida means by denying the present, and subsequently and related to this the denial of a something which is perceived– 'I don't believe that there is any perception'[3] – we need to return to Derrida's technique of deconstruction and the conclusions that he draws from this.

We have seen that Husserl tried to isolate a world of expression, a world of pure meaning, which was not sullied by indication. Derrida tries to show two things. First, that Husserl's distinction does not hold because indication can never be successfully excluded from expression: 'indicative functions . . . continually reappear . . . and getting rid of them will be an infinite task'.[4] We should repeat that this is not an attack on a particular distinction. For Derrida it is merely an example of his wider claim that all distinctions could be deconstructed in this manner. One of the reasons why Derrida chose to deconstruct this particular distinction is that the disintegration of this distinction indicates why all distinctions must fall. Derrida's argument is that signs cannot refer to something totally other than themselves. His demonstration that an expression must involve indication implies that there is no pure meaning that can be abstracted from the sign. Signs are not transparent; they are not simply marks for something which is wholly other. Put in the language of semiology, there is no signified which is independent of the signifier. There is no realm of meaning which can be isolated from the marks which are used to point to it. There is therefore no logos, no unified and coherent account of the world, that lies outside the sign or system of signs, that is independent of the marks by which 'it' is described.

Derrida's claim that the signified cannot be separated from the signifier is the prelude to a much wider and more significant claim. Having argued that there cannot be a realm of the signified independent of the signifier, he goes on to argue that the distinction itself is untenable:

From the moment that one questions the possibility of such a transcendental signified, and that one recognizes that every signified is also in the position of a signifier, the distinction between signified and signifier becomes problematical at its root.[5]

Without the possibility of an independent signified Derrida opens up the vista of an endless play of signifiers that refer not to signifieds but to other signifiers. Another way of putting this is to say that for Derrida meaning is always ultimately undecidable.

Derrida cannot, however, be regarded as presenting a theory of signs in the simplistic form that we have just outlined. Such a theory would reflexively undermine itself, for it would be a theory of signs that claimed that there could be no such theory. In order to have the character of a theory it would have to have a decidable meaning, which is precisely what it denies. Thus Derrida's method is to deconstruct Husserl's theory of signs in order to deny the possibility of a logos, of a unifying account, without himself having to assert a theory which would inevitably imply the existence of a logos. The deconstruction of Husserl's distinction is thus a means of showing that the assumption of a logos (a position that Derrida describes as logocentrism), is not tenable.

The second point that Derrida makes is that logocentrism, and the belief that it is possible to provide an account of the world in a final or definitive way, is based on the assumption that the present is accessible. Thus Husserl's pure expression is immediately available to consciousness – meaning is immediately present to itself. Derrida's demonstration that there cannot be a pure expression is intimately linked to his argument that there cannot be a pure presence, for it is through the idea of the present that philosophers have been able to uphold the possibility of providing a unified account of the world.

Derrida's denial of the present can be regarded as an outcome of his analysis of language – and in particular of Husserl's theory of the sign. While Derrida's style of writing does not take the form of presenting a case and then supporting it with rigorous argument, nevertheless he can be interpreted as drawing two conclusions from his analysis of Husserl's theory of the sign which result in his denunciation of the metaphysics of presence. Having argued that a realm of the independent signified is not possible Derrida concludes first, that no particular sign can be regarded as referring to any particular signified, and second, that we are unable to escape the system of signifiers. In combination these conclusions imply that there can be no presence. For if our world is held within the play of signifiers, and if any particular signifier fails to have a unique meaning, then all meaning is undecidable, and since there is only meaning, there is nothing outside meaning – there can be no presence.

Having attempted to demonstrate that there is no presence, Derrida is then able to argue that the history of philosophy is the result of philosophers trying to maintain presence in the face of impossible odds. The priority that has been given to speech over writing, which Derrida calls phonocentrism, is a result of the assumption of presence. Speech has been regarded as prior because it is closer to the possibility of presence. It is closer because speech implies immediacy, in speech meaning is apparently immanent, above all when, using the inner 'voice' of consciousness, we speak to ourselves. In the moment of speech we appear to grasp its meaning, and are thereby able to capture presence, as if it was given, finally decided, once and for all.

Thus unlike writing, which is hopelessly mediated, speech is linked to the apparent moment and place of presence, and for this reason has been prioritized over writing. For Derrida, therefore, phonocentrism is one of the effects of the metaphysics of presence. His attempts to deconstruct the opposition between speech and writing is therefore linked to the uncovering of the metaphysics of presence as a whole.

If Derrida had said of poetry that its meaning was undecidable, this would not have been regarded as a very radical claim. It is almost self-evident that there are a variety of possible interpretations of any given poem. For this reason, Derrida argues, philosophers have been suspicious of writing – a written text is more capable of dissimulation, of being unclear in its meaning. In denying presence, and in denying the possibility of a decidable meaning, Derrida is introducing the play which we expect of poetry into the most precise and elementary statements.

Thus for Derrida the most banal statement of the form 'the chair is black' has an undecidable meaning. Its meaning is undecidable because 'the chair is black' does not refer to some independent entity, namely the black chair. The meaning of his denial of presence in this instance would be that we are not able to prove the truth of the statement 'the chair is black' by going to look at the chair, for there is no present experience which provides the data against which we can check the statement. There are no data because there is no pure presence. The 'ideal' raw data are beyond our reach – all we have is a collection of meanings, and even then there are no fixed meanings. There is no independent signified, the signified being always merely part of the play of the signifiers.

For a moment it may appear that Derrida is adopting some wildly idealist position in denying the existence of reality. In fact, Derrida tends to describe his own position rather inversely, as a type of radical empiricist. For he is not saying that we cannot be certain that there is a chair that is black, in the sense of doubting the existence of the external world. Rather he is saying that there is no single definitive meaning of the sentence 'the chair is black', and that there is no single meaning to our experience at any point. The meaning of a sentence takes place in the play that is the web of language, and experience is not an independent thing which stands outside that play.

Derrida's analysis of Husserl thus accounts for Husserl's theory in the light of his logocentrism and the metaphysics of presence. In searching for that which is immediately and thus uncontestably present, Husserl prioritizes first speech over writing, and then the internal voice of consciousness over the speech of communication. This, Derrida argues, is because in the voice that we use to think to ourselves there is no mediation; we are juxtaposed to the present meaning: 'The voice is the being which is present to itself in the form of universality, as consciousness; the voice *is* consciousness.'[6] But it is precisely in this highpoint of pure presence, Derrida argues, that the indicative aspect of the sign enforces itself, and thus even in the way that consciousness is present to itself there is non-presence, or absence. Deconstruction is possible because the text is written on the assumption of a decidable meaning and the metaphysical presupposition of presence. This decidability can be broken down by returning to the necessary tension between presence and absence.

In much the same way that Heidegger took issue with the tradition of the West and denounced philosophers since Parmenides for being metaphysical, Derrida argues that almost all previous philosophers have succumbed to the metaphysics of presence. Speech, carrying with it the immediacy of presence, was life, while writing was a destructive, sinister influence that threatened the purity of speech. In order to limit the danger held within writing, it was reduced to being almost nothing– the signifier of the signifier. Writing signified speech which signified the idea. Writing was thus seen as secondary to speech, subsequent upon the real presence which is found in the voice. Derrida plays on the paradoxical position of writing– that on the one hand it is seen to be nothing, a mere secondary reduplication of the origin, and yet it has to be completely other so that the pure presence of speech is not contaminated by the undecidability of writing. In arguing that speech is always bound up with writing Derrida is therefore saying that presence is always bound up with absence.

By taking issue with the privilege that we have traditionally assigned to the now, and thereby to the possibility of decidable meaning, Derrida is in a certain way removing the very subject of philosophy:

Within philosophy there is no possible objection concerning this privilege of the present-now; it defines the very element of philosophical thought, it is evidence itself, conscious thought itself, it governs every possible concept of truth and sense. No sooner do we question this privilege than we begin to get at the core of consciousness itself from a region that lies elsewhere than philosophy, a procedure that would remove every possible security and *ground* from discourse. In the last analysis what is at stake is indeed the privilege of the actual present, the now. This conflict, necessarily unlike any other, is between philosophy, which is always a philosophy of presence, and a meditation on nonpresence – which is not perforce its contrary, or necessarily a meditation on a negative absence, or a theory of nonpresence *qua* unconsciousness.[7]

If Derrida is arguing for the abandonment of presence, of decidable meaning and of philosophy, what is he saying we should put in its place? If we have been caught within the confines of logocentrism and the metaphysics of presence, how are we to break out?

Writing and différance

In his criticism of logocentrism and the metaphysics of presence, and thus of speech, decidable meaning, and pure origin, Derrida finds himself necessarily propounding an alternative account. At its most banal it is simply a question of asserting the opposite. Instead of stressing speech and presence, Derrida accentuates writing and absence. This is, however, only a superficial effect, and a conclusion that Derrida explicitly warns us against. 'Of course it is not a question of "rejecting" these notions; they are necessary and, at least at present, nothing is conceivable for us without them.'[8] Instead he appears to make a typically Hegelian move whereby presence necessarily involves absence, and speech is always already bound up with writing. Having used reflexivity as a critical weapon, Derrida now can be seen to incorporate reflexivity into the terms which provide the alternative 'theory'.

So far we have been referring to 'writing' in its normal sense. Rather confusingly, however, Derrida most commonly uses 'writing' in a very different sense. (To say that there is a normal sense, or even to say that there is a sense on any particular occasion, is of course to have already adopted a logocentric position; but, as Derrida warns, to move too quickly is to risk destroying the text altogether.) Derrida sometimes refers to this special sense of 'writing' as 'arche-writing'. It is the 'source' from which the opposition of speech and writing comes forth. Thus speech is always already writing, not in the sense that it has always been written graphically, but in that it is already bound into the network of signifiers that takes it beyond the pretended purity of its 'immediately present meaning'. It is writing in this sense that escapes the metaphysics of presence, for instead of the meaning of a sign being immediately present, it is disseminated throughout the entire network of signifiers, thus allowing the opposition of both presence and absence.

Writing, or arche-writing, in this Derridean sense is thus the prerequisite of both speech and writing. We have described this new sense of writing as a core from which the opposition of speech and writing (in the graphic sense) can break out. But if this is what Derrida meant by writing, it would immediately find itself within the logocentric tradition. Writing would have taken on the character of something potentially present, something that was once present – the origin of an opposition. One might think that the next step would be to consider writing not as the origin of the opposition of speech and writing, but as the opposition itself. This comes no closer to being a solution, however, for it would still be an attempt to provide a final account of the structure of language, and as such would be part of a logocentric perspective.

Derrida uses the concept of 'writing' to try to escape the confines of logocentrism. Yet as soon as this concept is fixed it only serves to reassert logocentrism. The destructive aspects of reflexivity, which Derrida employs to such effect against others, can here be seen to threaten the Derridean account itself. However, rather than try to avoid this reflexive paradox, Derrida takes it on board and uses the very unsettling effect of the reflexive move as the means to escape logocentrism. Derrida's technique is to allow, indeed to encourage, reflexivity to shake the description of writing that he himself has given and thereby avoid providing a final account.

Derrida can thus be seen to give us a picture of writing as the arche-writing from which both speech and graphic writing can emerge, which is itself beyond the logos. This 'writing' is thus both the source of presence and the destruction of the possibility of that presence.

The 'rationality' – but perhaps that word should be abandoned for reasons that will appear at the end of this sentence – which governs a writing thus enlarged and radicalized, no longer issues from a logos. Further it inaugurates the destruction, not the demolition but the de-sedimentation, the de-construction, of all the significations that have their source in that of the logos. Particularly the signification of truth.[9]

This image of writing cannot, however, remain if it is to take account of its own reflexive impact. A concept that does not have its source in the logos cannot allow itself to be described in this manner, for to do so would be to take part in that logos. It is not sufficient to be merely antagonistic to the logos, to escape its clutches. There is, in the attempt to describe 'writing' the failure to do so. If the description were achieved, 'writing' would have been placed, however subtly and self-denyingly, in the logocentric structures of our present thought. For this reason the science of the gramme– grammatology– harbours within it its own impossibility.

A science of writing runs the risk of never being established as such and with that name. Of never being able to define the unity of its project or its object. Of not being able either to write its discourse on method or to describe the limits of its field.[10]

Faced with this origin which cannot be an origin, with this non-absence which is not simply presence, one of Derrida's responses is to oscillate from giving us apparently straightforward descriptions of 'writing' to denying the possibility of doing any such thing. Although Derrida appears to allow 'writing' to become a pure, negative concept – 'It is that very thing which cannot let itself be reduced to the form of *presence*'[11] – he retains its apparently specific content, which is associated with his account of the history of graphic writing. By playing on the difference and similarity of arche-writing and graphic writing Derrida makes it more difficult for the reader to provide a unitary meaning for 'writing'; but it is above all through allowing the reflexive paradox held within writing to take place that he avoids any final description of this term. Thus as 'the very thing which cannot let itself be reduced to the form of presence' it would have reduced itself to the form of presence – it would be 'that very thing'. This paradoxical formulation is not a mistake – it is Derrida's means of avoiding the assertion of a final description. Without incorporating reflexivity into 'writing', 'writing' as a simply negative concept would in its negativity have acquired the characteristics of presence.

If despite all of these moves (some might say evasions), Derrida found himself arguing that beyond logocentrism and the metaphysics of presence there was 'writing', he would only have served to reintroduce God or Being– forms of presence– by another term. In one of his early essays he does say 'Writing is the moment of this original Valley of the other within Being',[12] but later he employs criticisms of Heidegger that would equally apply to this remark. In order to avoid portraying 'writing' as the origin beyond logocentrism, Derrida introduces a number of other terms to describe this non-originary origin.

One of Derrida's most central terms is 'différance'. Like 'writing' this concept reflexively incorporates in itself the denial that it is itself. At the moment that we take 'différance' to mean one thing it eludes that meaning and 'differs' from it. To understand the oppositions that are held within the space which is marked out by 'différance' we can only look at the variety of contexts in which it has been used. Certainly, 'différance' could not be adequately placed in a dictionary, for any summary account of its meaning must, in principle, have missed the mark.

Although 'différance' spelt with an 'a' is a term initiated by Derrida, a similar term had previously been used by Heidegger in his essay 'Language' published in 1959. 'The intimacy of world and thing is present in the separation of the between; it is present in the dif-ference.'[13] Dif-ference is for Heidegger the means by which world and thing come into being in relationship to one another. It is not simply the unity of the opposition of world and thing, but the means by which the two aspects of the opposition can come into being at all. Furthermore it is language that brings forth dif-ference, and through dif-ference the unity of the opposition of world and things. 'Language speaks. Its speaking bids the dif-ference to come which expropriates world and things into the simple onefold of their intimacy.'[14]

Derrida's term 'différance' has much in common with this Heideggerian use of 'dif-ference'. For Heidegger, dif-ference is both related to language – for it is that which language calls forth, and it is also that which makes possible the elements and the relationship of the opposition world and thing. Derrida also uses 'différance' in these two contexts. Différance is both that which enables the opposition of presence and absence to take place, and the non-originary origin that allows the play of the signifier and the signified. Here in the concept of différance we can see linked Derrida's analysis of language and his 'theory' of the metaphysics of presence.

As we have seen, Derrida's analysis of Husserl led him to portray language as an endless play of signifiers. Once an independent signified was abandoned signifiers referred to other signifiers which yet again referred to signifiers. Since there is nothing wholly other in this economy, what provides its content is difference. Each signifier differs from every other; differs in the way in which it is linked into the whole network of signifiers, and differs in that its use on any occasion is always in opposition to other signifiers. This difference is that which enables the signifier to have content. Language is thus the play of differences which are generated by signifiers which are themselves the product of those differences.

'Différance' is this play of differences. But it is also that which enables the play of differences to take place. For Derrida speech is necessarily already a writing because the immediate presence of meaning is already bound into the network of signifiers and thus to that which is not present. Différance is that which enables language to take place by allowing this opposition between speech and writing to occur. It is therefore not only the differences that occur within the system of language but the place from which these differences are themselves made possible. 'Différance will be not only the play of differences within the language but the relation of speech to language, the detour by which I must also pass in order to speak.'[15]

For Derrida there is no residue left over from meaning which would provide consciousness with content. This play of differences, of the network of signifiers, is all that there is. It is for this reason that Derrida makes the claim that 'there is nothing outside of the text'. This claim has a wider meaning than simply to say that in the reading of a text we should not take into account anything extraneous. For Derrida would wish to say of life 'there is nothing outside of the text'. There is nothing beyond the play of differences of the signifiers. There is no 'real' experience, no pure consciousness. At an ontological level there is no realm that does not lie within the play of the signifiers. 'All experience is the experience of meaning. Everything that appears to consciousness, everything that is for consciousness in general, is *meaning*.'[16] For this reason, therefore, différance, by being that which allows language and the opposition of speech and writing to take place, is also that which enables presence and absence. For there is no presence and absence outside language. Différance, in enabling the opposition of presence and absence, is not a further presence that lies behind presence and absence, but a non-originary origin that enables presence and non-presence to occur.

We have described two aspects of différance, and yet it could be said that 'différance' was wholly different from these descriptions. For 'différance', in trying to name that which allows the play of differences within language, cannot itself escape that play of differences. 'Différance', in being the source of the elements and the opposition of presence and absence, cannot itself avoid that opposition of presence and absence, In being articulated, therefore, différance fails to 'describe' what it is seeking to 'describe'. It is for this reason that Derrida spells 'différance' with an 'a'.

'Différance' draws on two aspects of the French verb *differer*: one of these is 'to differ', to be unequal, to be different; the other is 'to defer', to put off, to postpone. These two aspects Derrida portrays as contradictory; 'in the one case "to differ" signifies nonidentity; in the other case it signifies the order of the *same*'[17] (the order of the same, because in deferring we put off until later what is not possible now). 'Différance' would normally be a misspelling in French, just as 'differance' would be a misspelling in English. On a first level, Derrida wishes to use this misspelling to incorporate into the sense of 'difference' the sense of deferring. In deferral that which apparently could be present is kept back. Thus deferral contains within it the assumption of presence, but a presence that is not present. It is for this reason that Derrida can say 'We provisionally give the name *différance* to this *sameness* which is not *identical* . . . .' This misspelling, however, does more than incorporate another sense into difference. It does not allow the concept to rest, for 'différance' is neither the difference between the oppositional concepts within language, nor is it the deferring through which the opposition of writing and speech is made possible. Within 'différance' are held both of these senses. Furthermore, 'différance' differs from 'différence' in a way that can only be discerned graphically – in speech the two words are pronounced identically. Thus in 'différance' Derrida demonstrates his thesis that discourse necessarily involves the intervention of a written sign. But while 'différance' is all of these things, it also differs from itself. 'Différance' is itself endlessly differed. We move towards an idea of différance, but the centre of différance is always somewhere else. 'Différance' is both deferred from itself, and different from itself, a presence which is endlessly postponed, and that which is not what it is. Thus while Derrida uses the term 'différance' in all of these varied but linked contexts, and while at times he appears to be saying that 'différance' is such and such, he also says:

There is no essence of différance; not only can it not allow itself to be taken up into the *as such* of its name or its appearing, but it threatens the authority of the *as such* in general, the thing's presence in its essence.[18]

'Différance' would appear to be caught in a reflexive paradox, caught within the web of signifiers and presence and yet wishing to stand outside of them. It is, however, this very paradox which Derrida incorporates into 'différance', a paradox that is made explicit by the evident tension introduced by the silent 'a'. As a result Derrida is led to say: 'Différance produces what it forbids, makes possible the very thing that it makes impossible.'[19] The process of differing can never be halted and thus even this formulation must be overthrown. 'Différance' must differ from itself, whatever that 'itself' maybe. Here we see reflexivity not in a destructive role, but as the motor which determines the character of the 'theory' which Derrida provides. The reflexive whirlpool that Derrida has here led us into he calls an aporia, a paradox that is not to be avoided but which is unfathomable.

'Writing' and 'différance' have a similar form in the way that they both efface themselves. Derrida incorporates a reflexivity which eventually seems to leave only a vortex of undecidability. There are other terms in Derrida's vocabulary which take on a similar role. 'Trace' and 'supplement' are such 'concepts'. Like 'writing' and 'différance' they have their origins in meanings that can be explicated. 'Trace' is a term that Derrida uses to indicate that through which anything has meaning. It is not therefore presence – for there is no presence, but it is that in virtue of which there is not nothing. One might say that différance is made up of traces – but then *'the (pure) trace is différance'*.[20] Inevitably the trace has the same aporetic character as différance. *'The trace is in fact the absolute origin of sense in general. Which amounts to saying once again that there is no absolute origin of sense in general . . . .'*[21]

The supplement is initially that which has to be added to speech. While writing has been seen as a mere supplement, a sort of invisible addition to speech, Derrida argues that it is essential. The supplement, instead of being seen as a transparent token, is seen to be the source. 'One wishes to go back *from the supplement to the source*: one must recognize that there is a *supplement at the source*.'[22] If Derrida's subsequent remarks about the supplement sound familiar – 'Less than nothing and yet, to judge by its effects, much more than nothing.

The supplement is neither a presence nor an absence. No ontology can think its operation'[23] – this is not by accident, for supplement is 'another name for différance'.[24]

The glimpse beyond and the parody of parody

We might say of writing, différance, trace and supplement that they are all names for the same thing. Yet there would be an absurdity in such a remark, for it is 'essential' to these terms that there is no 'thing' that they are naming. All of them take part in the play of signifiers; they were chosen strategically because of the echoes that they had at the time Derrida was writing. Derrida expresses these thoughts in his typically elliptical style:

This common root, which is not a root but the concealment of the origin and which is not common because it does not amount to the same thing except with the unmonotonous insistence of difference, this unnameable movement of *difference-itself*, that I have strategically nicknamed *trace, reserve*, or *différance*, could be called writing only within the historical closure, that is to say within the limits of science and philosophy.[25]

These terms are not definitive, but rather provide Derrida with a mechanism to break open the closure of our metaphysics.

Why of the *trace*? What led us to the choice of this word? . . . If words and concepts receive meaning only in sequences of differences, one can justify one's language, and one's choice of terms, only within a topic (an orientation in space) and an historical strategy. The justification can therefore never be absolute and definitive.[26]

Moreover, although Derrida uses these terms to escape from the strictures of logocentrism, and although they incorporate within them many tricks to avoid their reflexive annihilation, they are an attempt to name the unnameable. Towards the end of his essay 'Différance' Derrida writes

'Older' than Being itself, our language has no name for such a différance. But we 'already know' that if it is unnameable, this is not simply provisional; it is not because our language has still not found or received this *name*. . . . It is because there is no *name* for this, not even essence or Being – not even the name 'différance', which is not a name . . . .[27]

109

In so far as these terms différance, writing, trace, and supplement are attempts to name the unnameable they are, once used, also disposable. Each pushes up against the limits of meaningfulness as successive layers of reflexivity are added and the term becomes more and more unstable. Each is used to venture forth out of the metaphysics of presence, by characterizing a something which does not find itself within the metaphysics of presence. Each subsequently finds itself inevitably caught within the present web of language, a web that is logocentric and carries within it the metaphysics of presence. Although Derrida spends much time elucidating these terms, once used they are nevertheless to be abandoned – for the point of the structures that they set up is to demolish all structures including their own. This is the third aspect of reflexivity which we can discern in Derrida's writing: his own texts turning back on themselves and erasing their own claims, however much reflexivity has already been incorporated in those claims.

If Derrida is to be seen denouncing the story of the metaphysics of presence, the first story with which he replaces it, the story of writing, différance, trace and supplement, is a story that evaporates in the telling. But it is not then reduced to nothing, for it provides a framework, an economy of terms, which Derrida is able to call on in order to shake logocentrism. These and other terms such as 'force', 'brisure', 'spur', are used to push out against the strictures of presence, to bring the assumption of presence to our notice. They are not trying to present an alternative other – for they cannot be trying to 'present' anything. They shake the foundations without proposing a new building.

It can now be seen why deconstruction is both the basis for Derrida's 'theory' of the metaphysics of presence and the result of that theory. From a deconstruction of Husserl's theory of signs Derrida develops his account of logocentrism and the metaphysics of presence. This account is supported by further deconstructions which could in principle be applied to any text. The 'theory', however, reflexively dissolves itself, since it cannot allow itself to stand, to be present. We might say that Derrida's own theory deconstructs itself. As a result the theory brings us back to deconstruction once again. Deconstruction is thus more than a method that leads us to a conclusion – for the conclusion itself leads us back to deconstruction. It is for this reason that Derrida's writing is often a combination of 'theory' and deconstructive reading. *Of Grammatology* is explicitly of this form – divided into two parts: the theory and the application. Theory and deconstruction are thus entwined, each being both the source and the product of the other.

If Derrida is not asserting his theory of logocentrism, both in the sense that he does not claim it to be definitively true, and also in the sense that there is no thing that has an identity that is being asserted, what is he doing? In response to this question Derrida makes a number of moves, which can be subsumed under two general themes. One of these is the glimpse beyond, and the other is the parody of parody. The glimpse beyond arises from Derrida finding himself first within what he would call the closure of knowledge – within the constraints of the epoch of logocentrism – and then engaging in methods to escape this closure. One form of attempt at escape is erasure– the crossing through and erasing of a word written in the text. This technique had already been used by Heidegger for a similar purpose. The function of the erasure is to allow the term to be asserted but simultaneously to retract it. One might say that what is left is the trace. Derrida also uses inverted commas or italic writing to indicate erasure. Heidegger applied erasure to his central terms such as Being, but for Derrida the whole of the text finds itself caught within the closure of knowledge and therefore he uses erasure more widely. It is through erasure that Derrida tries to explain how we are to understand the term 'différance'.

Différance . . . can however, be thought of in the closest proximity to itself only on one condition: that one begins by determining it as the ontico-ontological difference before erasing that determination. The necessity of passing through that erased determination, the necessity of that 'trick of writing' is irreducible.[28]

One way of describing Derrida's writing as a whole is to say that it all takes place under erasure, and does so in order to avoid the closure of knowledge, in order to demonstrate that it is not to be taken as an assertion. 'As for the concept of experience, it is most unwieldy here. Like all the notions I am using here, it belongs to the history of metaphysics and we can only use it under erasure.'[29]

The significance of erasure is that although it retracts what is at once asserted, what is left is not nothing. It is an attempt to glimpse beyond the closure of knowledge. Some of Derrida's other moves to explain what he is up to are related to this glimpse of a world outside of the closure of knowledge. To escape the confines of our present attitude we require new names, names that are not placed within the space of our present network of signifiers.

As for what 'begins' then – 'beyond' absolute knowledge – *unheard-of* thoughts are required, sought for across the memory of old signs. As long as we ask if the concept of differing should be conceived on the basis of presence or antecedent to it, it remains one of these old signs, enjoining us to continue indefinitely to question presence within the closure of knowledge.[30]

And yet while there is a search for new thoughts they will not be held within the frame of a name. It is this criticism that Derrida levels at Heidegger. Any name must find its place within logocentrism, and therefore however dissimulating the name, however much crossed-out and denied, it must still present itself as knowledge, and thereby take part in the metaphysics of presence. For this reason Derrida does not allow any of his terms to aspire to being names. 'What we do know, what we could know if it were simply a question of knowing, is that there never has been and never will be a unique word, a master name.'[31] What Derrida does, however, is to supply us with a series of names, all of which deny their status as names, and furthermore are actually seen to do so in that they are later abandoned.

Erasure and the provision of new 'names' can be regarded as only a part of a wider Derridean aim. In so far as we find ourselves within the epoch of the closure of knowledge, Derrida implies that this epoch is drawing to a close. The technique of deconstruction and the unsettling of the metaphysics of presence with the use of such terms as 'différance' are means of moving towards a new 'epoch' which will no longer be bound by the closure of knowledge. For the moment we can only operate from within logocentrism, but we can glimpse the closure of the epoch, and catch the possibility of a language without knowledge.

The unity of all that allows itself to be attempted today through the most diverse concepts of science and of writing is, in principle, more or less covertly yet always, determined by an historical-metaphysical epoch of which we merely glimpse the *closure*.[32]

Deconstruction is therefore the means by which one operates from the 'inside' in order to reach an 'outside'. Derrida is unable to stand somewhere else and explain how the change is going to come about–

for there is nowhere else to stand; we are, of necessity, here. Deconstruction, by unsettling the theories with which we have surrounded ourselves, serves to indicate that our account of the world could be different – it cannot tell us how it will be different. In the process deconstruction is able gradually to shift the structures within which we operate – as if one day we might awake and find ourselves in a new era, beyond the closure of knowledge. Derrida is not suggesting that there will be sudden moment of revolution, an 'epistemological break' that will yield a new era, but rather a gradual modifying of the structures within which we operate, 'little by little to modify the terrain of our work, and thereby produce new configurations'.[33]

One of the problems that faces Derrida is that if he necessarily finds himself within logocentrism, how are any of these glimpses of a beyond possible? What distinguishes a Derridean deconstruction from a text that stands squarely within the metaphysics of presence? Derrida's reply to these two questions implicitly relies on a distinction between what a text says and what a text can show. The glimpse of a beyond is made possible through the reflexive returning of the text to itself, for in this movement the present meaning is shaken and is shaken in a way that cannot simply be thrown off. 'Once the circle turns, once the volume rolls itself up, once the book is repeated, its identification with itself gathers an imperceptible difference which permits us efficaciously, rigorously, that is, discretely, to exit from closure.'[34] Thus the move of reflexivity allows the text to indicate in the shift of meaning that there is something beyond what is merely said.

Something invisible is missing in the grammar of this repetition. As this lack is invisible and undeterminable, as it completely redoubles and consecrates the book, once more passing through each point along its circuit, nothing has budged. And yet all meaning is altered by this lack. Repeated, the same line is no longer exactly the same, the ring no longer has exactly the same centre, *the origin has played*.[35]

Since the Derridean text is not able to say that it is different from a text that stands within the metaphysics of presence, Derrida allows his text to leave a track which indicates what it is trying to do. This pathway is not something that we are told of within the text, but is something that is shown in the structure of the text through its reflexive movement – if it was possible to say what it is that is shown in the structure it would not be necessary, and therefore an attempt to explain this pathway here would be absurd. Without it, however, Derrida would have trapped himself so tightly within the metaphysics of presence that he could not escape – and even if he had escaped we could not know. 'Without that track, abandoned to the simple content of its conclusions, the ultra-transcendental text will so closely resemble the pre-critical text as to be indistinguishable from it.'[36]

Once reduced to the 'track' or the 'pathway', however, this attempt to prise open the closure of knowledge to allow for an indication of the beyond is as inevitably caught up in the closure of knowledge as the other terms employed by Derrida. Both 'track' and 'pathway' are spatial metaphors, of a type typical of the metaphysics of presence. So for that matter is the term 'beyond'. If the text is to indicate by its form something other than that which it immediately says, it is not susceptible to being reduced to something that is 'said' in the text. If the movement of reflexivity unsettles the reader and has an effect in addition to the impact of any portion of the text taken in isolation, this effect, meaning, or glimpse, cannot be described – for to describe it would be to place it within the text, and thereby to achieve immediately what is claimed cannot be achieved and what prompted the requirement for a 'pathway' in the first place. This may explain why, although an important aspect of his writing, Derrida's account of the functioning of the pathway or track is limited to little more than the odd remark.

The idea that the text can indicate something through its structure, is, like erasure and the concepts of writing and différance, a method of catching a glimpse of what lies beyond the closure of knowledge and the metaphysics of presence. All of these concepts enable Derrida to account for what he is doing in terms of the emergence of a new epoch, an epoch in which there is no present, and thus no history; an epoch which is no longer 'an epoch'. By unsettling the belief in presence, Derrida is able to catch a glimpse of a world without presence which escapes the strictures which he sees as having characterized the entire history of the west.

At times Derrida does undoubtedly give this explanation of his writing. He also characteristically denies such an explanation – for it is, of course, a description which remains firmly within our tradition. It could, however, be said to fall within a wider explanation that Derrida gives of his work. If presence and closure, track and pathway, writing and différance, are all necessarily linked to our present categories and forms of explanation, then there can be no beyond. Derrida is thus forced into saying that he is playing among the webs of language: parodying himself, and then parodying the parody. He is no longer trying to write of the end of the metaphysics of presence, for that description was itself just a play and parody of others. There is thus no centre of Derrida's writing; no sentence or portion of the text that can be considered the core of his thought. Nor is there a sentence which can be dismissed as being unimportant.

In his book *Spurs*, written in the early 1970s, Derrida considers Nietzsche's description of truth as 'a woman'. For Derrida, Nietzsche's 'woman' is a metaphor which operates at many different levels. Derrida formalizes these levels into three aspects. First, Nietzsche employs woman as the figure of falsehood, despised and censured in the name of truth and metaphysics. Second, Nietzsche writes deprecatingly of woman as the source not of falsehood but of truth; the fount of wisdom even if she is unaware of that truth and appears to deny it. Finally, woman is seen as an affirmative power beyond the opposition of truth and non-truth – affirming herself in her dissimulation. It is in this third sense that Nietzsche writes 'truth is a woman'. He does not, however, do so with the intention of asserting the character of truth once and for all. In this affirmation is held the dissembling character of that affirmation. It is only by incorporating the reflexive paradox within 'truth is a woman' that we can appreciate Nietzsche's remark.

The credulous and dogmatic philosopher who *believes* in the truth that is woman, who believes in truth just as he believes in woman, this philosopher has understood nothing. He has understood nothing of truth, nor anything of woman. Because indeed, if woman is truth, *she* at least knows that there is no truth, that truth has no place here and that no one has a place for truth. And she is woman precisely because she herself does not believe in truth itself, because she does not believe in what she is, in what she is believed to be, in what she thus is not.[37]

This description of Nietzsche's view of truth would equally apply to many Derridean terms. It would be possible to replace the term 'woman' in this quotation with 'writing', 'différance', 'trace', 'supplement', 'track' and so on. The characteristic of Nietzsche's truth is thus the characteristic of all of Derrida's writing.

Derrida does not leave his consideration of Nietzsche's 'truth' here. Derrida makes the point that Nietzsche's use of the metaphor of 'woman' and the play and parody of the levels held within it cannot involve a pure mastery of the text. If this were so, the technique could be described and followed. Here would be the possibility of a Nietzsche cult, a new religion that would devote itself to the cultivation of parody. In order to avoid this re-emergence of presence, within Nietzsche's text there must be a naïvety and lack of mastery. Although Derrida regards Nietzsche as the only philosopher to have avoided the metaphysics of presence, he is forced to say: 'Nietzsche himself did not see his way too clearly . . . Nietzsche might well be a little lost in the web of his text, lost much as a spider who finds he is unequal to the web he has spun.'[38] This is not said in any critical sense, but that, in order to preserve the playful character of the text, Nietzsche at play cannot know too clearly how that play operates. And, as Derrida himself plays with Nietzsche's text, he too must be 'a little lost', deceived by the webs in his own text; and since the reflexive move is ever-'present', in this instance he is a little deceived in regarding himself as 'a little lost'.

Derrida is thus in the position of regarding himself as being at play in the radical sense that the word 'play' is itself part of the play of difference. One of the consequences of this is that no particular term, or collection of terms, can provide a central role. Each part of the text is as significant as every other part. In the endless play and parody of signifiers there can be no hierarchy of importance. In illustration of this point Derrida considers a note found isolated in quotation marks in Nietzsche's unpublished manuscripts. 'I have forgotten my umbrella.'[39] It might be no more than a jotting to himself. It might have been a citation, or a phrase oveheard and noted for further use. We have no way of knowing what Nietzsche wanted to do with these words – or if he wanted to do anything. Perhaps they were meant to say nothing, or perhaps Nietzsche only pretended that they were of significance. The undecidability of the meaning of 'I have forgotten my umbrella' has nothing to do with our lack of understanding of the individual terms, or the complexity of the sentence structure. In one sense we all know what 'I have forgotten my umbrella' means, and yet we can have no idea of what its meaning is in this instance. We can imagine a reading in which the umbrella would be seen as a defence, as it is a defence from the weather. Thus Nietzsche on the verge of breakdown has left his defences behind: 'I have forgotten my umbrella': I am caught in the rainstorm. Or Derrida speculates it could be analysed in psychoanalytic terms, familiar as psychoanalysis is with forgetting and phallic objects. Such an analysis would assume that the fragment meant something, that it was part of a larger whole, and came from the depths of the author's thought. But Derrida has removed the possibility of it being part of a larger whole, and thus the possibility that the fragment means something particular, discernible through analysis. The origin of the text, like Nietzsche's umbrella, finds itself forgotten. Playfully Derrida remarks that it is 'a forgotten text. An umbrella perhaps'.[40] There is no limit to the potential play in this fragment; 'there is no end to its parodying play with meaning'.[41] And if Nietzsche meant to say something, could he not have meant just this limitlessness of meaning: caught in the open without any protection from the buffeting of other signifiers. When reflexivity is so completely endorsed there is no safety, no shelter from the elements, it is perhaps frightening as our defences have become no more than a memory: 'I have forgotten my umbrella.'

This illustration is used as a metaphor for the whole of Derrida's text. In the same way that the meaning of 'I have forgotten my umbrella' is immediately evident and yet totally absent, so is the entirety of Derrida's text. We can therefore ascribe no reason for Derrida's choice of this example. It may be no more than a joke on the philosophical world. It may be the kernel of his thought. It may be a coded message. Derrida encourages the text to evaporate as we play with it. 'There might yet be certain movements where the text, which already you are beginning to forget, could very well slip quite away. Should this indeed be the case, there would be no measure to its undecipherability.'[42]

Derrida is 'left in the position' of meaning to say nothing, and yet still saying something. In the webs of meaning, and the elliptical reflexive moves of the text, the endless parody cannot in the end come to anything; even parody is itself parodying. But still the text will remain – it will not finally evaporate despite all of its play. No matter how much Derrida tries to remove the text it will still insist.

117

The text will remain, if it is really cryptic and parodying (and I tell you that it is so through and through. I might as well tell you since it won't be of any help to you. Even my admission can very well be a lie because there is dissimulation only if one tells the truth, only if one tells that one is telling the truth), still the text will remain indefinitely open, cryptic, and parodying.[43]

Although we may therefore be tempted to ignore this maze of undecidable meanings and deem them simply meaningless, the text still returns and cannot be shrugged off. There remains a residue; a residue that cannot be copied – for there is nothing to copy – and yet cannot be ignored for it will not simply go away. The text is 'just an umbrella that you couldn't use'. We may think that we can abandon this umbrella 'either because it hasn't rained or else just because you don't like it',[44] but the forgotten umbrella that is Derrida's text cannot be simply abandoned even though 'it' means to say nothing.

It would be comforting if in a final paragraph Derrida could come to some conclusion. Faced with shifting sands that deny their character of shifting sand, we inevitably find ourselves imposing such an account on his text. We might say at this point, for example, that he constantly changes his metaphors in order to avoid any one of them solidifying into a single meaning, and that it is in the play of these metaphors that Derrida describes the workings of language and the world. Such an account and any other account tries to encapsulate and therefore 'give meaning to' a project whose aim is to avoid such encapsulation: although it is already absurd to say that it has an aim at all.

From a certain perspective, the reflexive paradoxes within Derrida's text wreak such havoc that they only serve to demonstrate the fallacy of his starting point. If the adoption of the view that 'meaning is undecidable' leads to the elimination of all conclusions and the inability to describe or prescribe any alternative, is this not a strong case for adhering to the view that meaning is decidable? From this outlook, if there are problems in providing a theory to account for the mechanisms which enable decidability, these are simply to be overcome and the alternative of abandoning decidability is not worth contemplating. Our efforts should therefore be directed towards providing a workable theory of language, and although our present accounts may be imperfect they are capable of being improved.

This possibility of providing a theory of language is precisely what is denied by Derrida. The rhetoric and manoeuvring within his writing are not merely speculative excess. The complexity and apparent chaos of Derrida's writing are the products of the view that an alternative that stands within the metaphysics of presence is not possible. His deconstruction of the writings of others seeks to demonstrate the impossibility of an alternative. Although the charge has been made, Derrida is not deliberately obtuse; he writes as he does because he does not regard it as possible coherently to adopt a stance within the metaphysics of presence, and any attempt to provide a theory of language must inevitably find itself within that tradition.

Despite the radical difference in style between Derrida and philosophers of language within the Anglo-Saxon, analytic, tradition, there are similarities that can be drawn between Derrida and the writings of the later Wittgenstein. In his early work, the *Tractatus Logico Philosophicus*, Wittgenstein tried to provide a general account of the relationship between language and the world. He subsequently abandoned this attempt, arguing that general philosophical claims were not possible and that all that was to be done was to examine the specifics of the way language was used and thereby eradicate philosophical problems. Derrida, with his use of style and his talk of the play of differences, is operating within the interstices of language in a manner not wholly different from that of the later Wittgenstein. Both philosophers refuse to make general philosophical claims, and both avoid providing an overall account of the purpose of their writing. Both adopted this approach of operating from the 'inside' as a result of rejecting a general theory of the relationship between language and the world – in Derrida's case Husserl's theory of signs, and in Wittgenstein's his own early work.

Despite the similarities between Wittgenstein and Derrida, it is perhaps in their differences that the comparison is most instructive. In concluding that general philosophical claims are not possible Wittgenstein does not then seek to find a method whereby a general philosophical outlook could be 'glimpsed'. Instead, he shifts the function of philosophy to a type of tidying-up operation, in which the aim is not to provide a complete world view, but to rid people of confusions which have led them to speculate pointlessly on such matters. Philosophers are seen to be people who have become obsessed with a certain set of problems, and Wittgenstein is providing a therapy whereby they can rid themselves of these delusions and escape back into ordinary life. In denying the possibility of general philosophical claims Wittgenstein also ceases to seek such claims – indeed he provides a therapeutic technique for those still haunted by such goals.

Derrida, however, in denying the possibility of an overall philosophical account of the world, appears still to seek to provide a glimpse of what such an account might look like, and in the process takes us through a number of different stages. While denying the possibility of presence, Derrida does not then adopt the Wittgensteinian move of abandoning the attempt to make general philosophical claims, but instead tries to circumvent the limitations of the metaphysics of presence. It is almost as if Derrida denies the possibility of an overall theory but unlike Wittgenstein nevertheless continues to try to provide one. Hence even in his denials of theory he reintroduces a theory in the form of 'tracks' and 'pathways'; even in the radical play of 'I have forgotten my umbrella' the meaning-to-say-nothing is still something.

We should not, however, conclude that Wittgenstein is rigorous, while Derrida illegitimately wishes to have it both ways. From a Derridean perspective Wittgenstein's denial of the possibility of general philosophical claims is no solution to the matter. To translate Wittgensteinian's assertion into Derridean language would be to say that it is not possible to achieve presence. Derrida, as we have seen, is unable to stop with this simple negative for reflexive reasons, for held within it is its own contradiction. In the very denial of presence there is the assertion of presence. Thus although Derrida wishes to abandon the metaphysics of presence he is endlessly caught up in it. Returning to the Wittgensteinian parallel the argument would be that to assert the impossibility of general philosophical claims is immediately to have made precisely the sort of general philosophical claim that is apparently being denied. Wittgenstein might well have argued that, for this reason, he avoided asserting even the mere negative. However, Wittgenstein did resort to metaphorical allusions in order to explain what he was trying to achieve. These descriptions are no less a general account by being metaphorical. Without some form of overview the remaining examples in Wittgenstein's writing would have little significance. Thus the reflexive criticism of Wittgenstein would be that Wittgenstein implicitly relies on a general theory, without which we would not know what to make of his text, while at the same time demonstrating the impossibility of that theory. Wittgenstein thus tries to hide from the paradoxes of reflexivity, which first appeared in the *Tractatus*, by simply ignoring them. For Derrida, there is no escape in this silence. Presence cannot be avoided by merely asserting non-presence or by evading any overt general statements. We find ourselves within the opposition of presence and absence, and no manoeuvring within that opposition can rid us of its tension.

So long as decidable meaning is thought to be possible, and so long as it is accepted that the 'here' and 'now' is immediately available, Derrida's writing can be relegated to the level of a misguided and irritating scepticism whose role is to sharpen the theoretical underpinning of our theories. But if meaning is not decidable, and if there is no presence, it is not apparent how this melée is to be avoided: rather more disturbing, perhaps, it is also not apparent where it leads. Derrida's abandonment of decidability would at first sight appear to imply the end of the search for knowledge and truth. Instead of trying to peer through the veil to see the truth beyond, we are to destroy the veil altogether. But such a description must reflexively carry within it that which it seeks to excise. For the metaphor of the veil appears to be the provision of a new truth. 'When it is a matter of the veil, is that not once again tantamount to unveiling? . . . This question *inasmuch as it is a question*, remains – interminably.'[45] The search for truth is not to be halted – for we do not know how this can be done. Our beliefs are shaken but they are not to be replaced with others. No theory is safe from the Derridean onslaught, but equally no theory is proclaimed. Yet theories of one form or another cannot be avoided.

There can be no final paragraph on Derrida, no way of ending the description of his text. The ever-implicit reflexive move will inevitably deny us that comfort. And yet, here we are, nearing the final paragraph of this chapter, the Derridean story almost told. It is as if we have recounted the story of the Book, and explained its paradox, and its ambiguity, and can thus rest content. No such manoeuvre is here claimed. Nor in a certain sense could the story of the Book ever have been told. Without the umbrella of knowledge to protect us from the ravages of undecidability, there can be no conclusion, even for ourselves, in this moment. This text itself has no pretensions to being such an umbrella.

It must be almost tautological to say that where such an end to ending leads is unclear. As Derrida concludes in the final essay of *Writing and Difference*:

What is to come is not a future present, yesterday is not a past present. The beyond of the closure of the book is neither to be awaited nor to be refound. It is *there*, but out there, *beyond*, within repetition, but eluding us there. It is there like the shadow of the book, the third party between the hands holding the book, the deferral within the now of writing, the distance between the book and the book, that other hand . . . . '*Tomorrow is the shadow and the reflexibility of our hands*'.[46]

Notes

1   J. Derrida, *Speech and Phenomena*, translated by David B. Allison (Northwestern University Press 1973), p. 20.
2   ibid., p. 50.
3   J. Derrida, *Structure, Sign and Play in the Discourse of the Human Sciences*, p. 272.
4   Derrida, *Speech and Phenomena*, p. 27.
5   J. Derrida, *Positions*, translated by Alan Bass (Athlone Press 1981), p. 20.
6   Derrida, *Speech and Phenomena*, pp. 79–80.
7   ibid., p. 62.
8   J. Derrida, *Of Grammatology*, translated by Gayati Spivak (Baltimore: Johns Hopkins University Press 1976), p. 13.
9   ibid., p. 10.
10 ibid., p. 4.
11 ibid., p. 57.
12 J. Derrida, *Writing and Difference*, translated by Alan Ball (Routledge and Kegan Paul 1978), p. 30.
13 M. Heidegger, *Poetry, Language, Thought*, translated by A. Hofstadster (Harper and Row 1971), p. 202.
14 ibid., p. 210.
15 Derrida, *Speech and Phenomena*, Essay on Difference, p. 146.
16 Derrida, *Positions*, p. 30.
17 Derrida, *Speech and Phenomena*, p. 129.
18 ibid., p. 158.
19 Derrida, *Of Grammatology*, p. 143.

20   ibid., p. 62.
21   ibid., p. 65.
22   ibid., p. 304.
23   ibid., p. 314.
24   ibid.
25   ibid., p. 93.
26   ibid., p. 70.
27   *Differance SP.* p. 159.
28   Derrida, *On Grammatology*, p. 23.
29   ibid., p. 60.
30   Derrida, *Speech and Phenomena*, p. 102.
31   *Differance SP*, p. 159.
32   Derrida, *On Grammatology*, p. 4.
33   Derrida, *Positions*, p. 24.
34   Derrida,*Writing and Difference*, p. 295.
35   ibid., p. 296.
36   Derrida, *On Grammatology*, p. 61.
37   J. Derrida, *Spurs*, translated by B. Harlow (University of Chicago Press 1978), p. 53.
38   ibid., p. 101.
39   ibid., p. 123.
40   ibid., p. 131.
41   ibid., p. 133.
42   ibid., p. 135.
43   ibid., p. 137.
44   ibid., p. 138.
45   ibid., p. 107.
46   Derrida, *Writing and Difference*, p. 300.

Further reading

Derrida has not written 'an introduction' to his work, nor has he provided us with an overview. That he has chosen not to do so is of course linked to his philosophical position. However, he comes closest to providing a theory in the first half of *Of Grammatology*, tr. G. Spivak (Johns Hopkins University Press 1976), and, in conjunction with the translator's introduction, one could do worse than begin here. Although *Speech and Phenomena, and Other Essays on Husserl's Theory of Signs*, tr. David Allison (Northwestern University Press 1973), is at times rather technical, it is also the basis from which all of Derrida's later works develop and is essential reading for those wishing to examine Derrida's work more closely. Of Derrida's more recent works *Spurs: Nietzsche's Styles*, tr. Barbara Harlow (Chicago, Ill: Chicago University Press 1979) illustrates most vividly the extent of Derrida's play with his own text.

The best introduction to Derrida is Christopher Norris's *Deconstruction: Theory and Practice* (Methuen 1982), which also includes a complete list of Derrida's translated works. De Man's, *Blindness and Insight: Essays in the Rhetoric of Contemporary Criticism* (New York and London: Oxford University Press 1971) was influential in developing the Derridean stance in the sphere of literary criticism. One should also mention Jonathan Culler's *Structuralist Poetics* (Routledge and Kegan Paul 1975), and *On Deconstruction* (Routledge and Kegan Paul 1983). The earlier of these two books is less sympathetic to the Derridean stance than the later one. A detailed bibliography for pre-1978 works can be found in John Leavey's and David B. Allison's, 'A Derrida Bibliography', in *Research in Phenomenology, VIII* (1978), p. 145–60.

Short introductory articles to Derrida that are to be recommended are Newton Garver's introduction to the English translation of Derrida's *Speech and Phenomena* which outlines some of the similarities between Derrida and Wittgensteinian philosophies of language; and Richard Rorty's marvellously clear article, 'Philosophy as a Kind of Writing', in *Consequences of Pragmatism* (Harvester Press 1982), which places Derrida, along with Wittgenstein and Dewey, in the non-Kantian tradition of conversational philosophy.

5

The rabbit?

To remain in the self-denying chaos generated by the *paradoxes* of reflexivity is not merely uncomfortble, but unsustainable. For this vortex annihilates all meaning. As a result those who have written in recognition of the impact of reflexivity can sometimes give the impression of an excessive self-consciousness, in which the text either appears to deny that which it asserts, or engages in systematic qualification – one might say hedging – to avoid making any assertions at all. Instead of a claim such as 'there is no certainty', we are provided with sentences of the form 'we could perhaps choose to say that there is no certainty, but we might equally choose to say that there must be certainty'. Such manoeuvring is unimpressive and risks vacuity; but to assert the chaos of the vortex is to risk madness.

There is only one choice: reflexivity in its paradoxical form must be avoided, or in some way contained. There are those who will argue that this is easily done; that the so-called paradoxes can either be eliminated altogether, or their impact limited. We have argued that such a simple alternative is not tenable. However hard one tries to squeeze out reflexive problems, they seem to reappear. Ironically, it is in the most rigorous texts that this is most obvious: Kant's *Critique of Pure Reason*, Wittgenstein's *Tractatus*, Husserl's *Logical Investigations*. Only in the texts of those who do not carry through the logic of their position is reflexivity apparently avoided. In such cases, however, it is simply submerged. The deconstructive technique employed by Derrida indicates that reflexive paradoxes can be found in any text, so long as they are examined closely.

Although reflexivity cannot be avoided in a direct way – by eliminating reflexive statements – this does not imply that the *paradoxes* of reflexivity have to be endorsed. While reflexivity cannot be eliminated it also cannot be allowed to destroy meaning. The importance of Nietzsche, Heidegger and Derrida is that they have all faced this dilemma. All have sought to harness reflexivity into a positive force, rather than to eradicate its destructive paradoxes. If they are deemed successful the apparent paradoxes cease to be destructive and become positive phenomena. One might say the paradoxes cease to be paradoxical.

The form of the impact of reflexivity in the texts of Nietzsche, Heidegger and Derrida is partly determined by the shift from a world of the individual subject to a world of the text. It is possible to see a development from Nietzsche to Derrida as the subject is gradually abandoned in favour of the text. In Heidegger one actually witnesses this transition in the change of emphasis from his early to his later writings. Yet the force of Nietzsche's reflexivity is due to his recognition of the all-embracing power of language, for questions of reflexivity are raised, in their modern form, once the relationship between language and the world is no longer seen simply as a form of mapping relationship. Even the bare statement 'the character of the world is to some extent determined by the concepts used to describe it', has an unsettling reflexive character. The seeds of such reflexive considerations were certainly present in Kant's linking of concepts and intuitions, and have strong parallels with Wittgenstein and the pragmatists Dewey and James. To reject the concern with reflexivity apparent in the writings of Nietzsche, Heidegger and Derrida, therefore, is to reject a significant proportion of so-called analytic philosophy as well.

While the predominant response of ignoring, or claiming to have evaded the problems of reflexivity is not sustainable, it is less clear whether Nietzsche, Heidegger and Derrida provide us with a satisfactory alternative. One can try to characterize the alternatives they offer: Nietzsche advocates anarchic assertion; Heidegger, endless postponement; and Derrida, perpetual unravelling. Each of these alternatives proposes a new mode of using language. In conjunction with this we are offered different notions of both truth and value. If we ask which of these alternatives is true we will inevitably make little headway. Nietzsche did not ask that we regard his views as true – in fact, he was more likely to insist that they were false, for to regard them as true would be to turn them to stone; Heidegger would deny that he ever arrived at the truth – we are always on the way, and being 'on the way' is itself on the way; while Derrida is lost in the texts of others, and in the text of his own making. How could being lost be true? In each case, although in different ways, there can be no end to their projects, nor in principle is it possible to give a final account of their views. Their writings cannot be reduced to the form of a theory which might be outlined in a text-book and learnt by students (although there are those who have attempted, and will attempt, to do so). There is therefore a sense in which to have characterized them at all is to have misled. (To guard ourselves against Nietzsche is also to guard ourselves against interpreting his writings as advocating anarchic assertion.)

We are therefore led to the question which above all a book about reflexivity cannot evade; a question which has silently determined many of the mannerisms and stylistic characteristics of this book. Is the description of reflexivity given in this text a true account? Is the interpretation of Nietzsche, Heidegger and Derrida accurate? Or have we here no more than a jumble of stories? These questions, and many others, follow from the central question of how the story of reflexivity outlined in this book, and illustrated in its chapters, and referred to in this sentence of this paragraph itself encounters its own reflexivity.

Although we hinted at this question in the beginning, we only ask it at the end. One might think that this is because it is an afterthought, a minor addition to an otherwise complete text. It is no such thing. The question is implicit throughout, but held in abeyance – for to speak too soon, and too loudly, is an ineffective rhetorical strategy. One might, for example, have added to many of the sentences in previous chapters a qualifying remark or a reflexive gesture – as if to say 'and this book too', 'and sentence too', 'and this phrase too' (and this sentence too). But it has been left unsaid, partly because it would be tedious to do otherwise, and partly because it would fail. (You may think the term 'tedious' a strange adjective to choose in this context. It seems so imprecise, so subjective. But the terms 'imprecise' and 'subjective' are the invective of the story of rationalism, which connives at pretending that these terms are not invective at all. If it would make you more comfortable, instead of saying 'it would be tedious' we could say 'the recurrent addition of qualifications would rapidly cease to have any impact on the reader'.) A more effective strategy is to maintain the fiction of truth – in a certain sense the fiction of truth can never be abandoned. In retrospect, however, with the story of reflexivity told, the question of the reflexivity of this text, and this story, can now be asked.

Perhaps, in response to the question, you are looking for an answer. But how is the rabbit to come out of the hat? How is the magician to carry off the trick? The audience wait, knowing that the trick is about to come. After all it has been announced. Yet if the trick is to work, not only must the audience remain ignorant of how the trick was done, but they should not even be aware that it was a trick at all. You are warned: there is no mere conjuring here.

If we draw Wittgenstein's rabbit on the page thus:

no one will deny that it is a rabbit, even if a magician can produce a duck instead. What was once a rabbit is now a duck, and just as we could describe the rabbit with its whiskers and its floppy ears, we can now describe the duck. And how has the magician achieved this? With the spell that is the word 'duck'. Are we not all magicians at play in the spells that we call language? Let us take another look at this rabbit that is not a rabbit, this duck that is not a duck. What else might it be? A drawing perhaps? Or a page in a book? What else can you, the readers of the text, the magicians, produce? You know when you look once again at this rabbit that is immediately not a rabbit what it is that you are trying to do, but how do you look for this new thing, that is not rabbit and not duck, not page and not drawing? As you look at this thing which is not anything in particular, before you know what it is going to be, it is held open.

Through language, theory, and text we close the openness that is the world. The closures we make provide our world – they are in a sense all that we have, and all that we could have. To want a final description of the world is to want more than this. We can provide many closures for our drawing – rabbit, duck, black lines on a white page, tiny particles impressed on a surface, analogy, and of course drawing. Is it not ridiculous to want only one of these to be the 'true' account? Or to imagine that one might come across the correct version? Or perhaps that we might add all the interpretations together and thereby achieve a complete account? And so it is with the world. We do not have different accounts of the same 'thing', but different closures and different things. At any given point many closures are possible but this does not mean that any of them will do, or that they are all the same. Far from it, they are all different. What matters is not that there are a multiplicity of possible closures but that each closure textures the world and thereby enables us to do things in the 'world'. The choice of closure is not a merely theoretical affair, for it determines the possibilities of action available to us. Closures not only provide a world but are the tools that enable one to deal with the world. And what of reflexivity? The closure 'closure' is itself a tool, an instrument. It is not an account of the world, a world that stands outside and beyond it, but is instead merely a locality, a place from which to operate.

Since this is not the place to elaborate a 'theory' of closure, let it suffice to say that this text tries to provide a closure, a place where one can be. To suggest that this is the only place to be would be laughable. As if there could be only one landscape painting, or one portrait! But this is not to say that this text is the same as all others, and of equal value. You may think that it resides in an unsatisfactory location – precarious, unclear and uncharted. Or you may think it desirable – a place where one can breathe. Do what you will with 'it', be it an umbrella, or a book, a rabbit or a closure, a critique or a philosophy. But do not believe that the world of the true and the false, the world of statues and idols – the fixed and immobile – can survive for long!

Acknowledgements

There are many to whom one owes thanks, but perhaps I will be forgiven if I mention only two. My close friend and colleague, Hugh Tomlinson, who at one stage was to have collaborated with me, suggested many revisions to draft versions of the book; but above all I would like to thank him for the numerous conversations, and arguments, we have had on the subject of reflexivity and related philosophical issues over the past decade. I would also like to thank Alan Montefiore for his advice and encouragement – without which the book might never have been written. The book is dedicated to the memory of my father, Harold Lawson.

Index